D.I.Y. – Detail It Yourself

The Car Enthusiast's Guide to a Fantastic Looking Car

Joey Monroe

D.I.Y. – Detail It Yourself : The Car Enthusiast's Guide to a Fantastic Looking Car

Copyright © 2016 by Joseph A. Monroe

Cover design by Jatin Aggarwal

ISBN: 9780692719022

First Edition: April 2016

10 9 8 7 6 5 4 3 2 1

CONTENTS

1

Introduction

Welcome to the world of Detailing!

Now, on to the reason you're even reading this book in the first place: Your Car. You love your car like a child (no offense to the kiddos, but it was probably here first anyway!). How you maintain your car is a reflection of you as a person. Your car is a mirror into your personality, your tastes, or even your culture. No one wants to be represented by a dingy, dirty, disheveled car, certainly not you, right?

By the end of this book, you will be armed with the expertise to keep your car (and others down the line) immaculate for years to come and have the pride of knowing YOU did that. Will you get the results of a talented, experienced detailer? Probably not. However, you also won't be paying the premium that a quality detailer commands!

Now, why did you choose my book in particular? I'll take you back to a few years when I first got my start: I got a car I really enjoyed and wanted to keep in great shape, so I dove head-first learning everything that I possibly could. The problem was; the information was scattered absolutely everywhere! Video sites, forums, social media groups and so on! Nevertheless, each detailer tends to fall into their own "brand" of habits and methods. This isn't necessarily a bad thing, but the methods they teach might be slightly outdated or not as effective as the newer innovations.

What did I do? I gleaned what I could, taking that advice with grains of salt. I tried and failed while attempting the various techniques, products, and tools. I learned a lot from this, but it took a long time! I was fortunate enough to stumble onto a mentor with a vast wealth of knowledge that I was able to learn even more through my time. Not everyone is so fortunate though!

Back to the question: Why did you choose my book? The resources out there are scattered, incomplete, or contradictory. I have made it my mission here to fit what I could in one place for you to be able to reference!

I'm going to make a promise to you here: If you read this book, understand and practice the principles, you WILL have incredible results for whatever vehicle you choose to use them on. Period. While I won't be able to cover every single possible scenario or condition, you should have a great arsenal of knowledge to use after this.

If you're a more visual learner and prefer to see the techniques in a video, stay tuned as I have a video course in the works!

So, don't be frustrated any longer! Don't put off reading this any longer! Follow me down the rabbit hole that is Detailing and come out on the other side, a lean mean detailing machine! (Totally not a polisher joke... okay, yes it was.)

Any techniques, tools or products used from this book are done so at your own risk, please follow product and technique instructions carefully, refer to the product MSDS sheets for full details about ingredients and risks. Don't overly exert yourself. Be sure to fully read and understand each chapter before you attempt them. Also, make sure to check your local municipality's environmental laws regarding water usage, chemical use and disposal, and above all, use common sense!

2

Most Common Mistakes

Over the years, there have been insane amounts of tips and tricks developed by your average Joe, old school hot rodders, professional detailers and the occasional misinformed good intention-er. Some have been accepted as "conventional wisdom" that end up with subpar results. Well, we aren't after subpar, now are we?

We are here to challenge those preconceptions using a mix of common sense, new technologies, best practices and an eye for detail. (No pun intended!)

So what are some of these common mistakes or misconceptions? I'll go over them one by one and then explain why they are wrong. I'll include the most common ones as this subject could be an entire book on its own! (Good idea, actually...)

Paint swirls: Just a byproduct of a clean car and unavoidable? Removed with a fresh coat of wax?

All nonsense. In reality, paint swirls are tiny scratches in your paint. For those of us with most modern cars post 1980's, this would be in the clear coat of your paint as demonstrated in the picture below. For those of you with classic cars that have single stage (base coat with no clear coat), the scratches reside directly in the base coat.

Swirls are the tiny valleys where paint has been dug into that you see in direct light. The light bounces off the valleys of the scratches and scatters, leading to a dull-looking finish and all the spider web-like lines you see in the paint.

They are most certainly avoidable using proper technique, wash medium, and proper care. This will all be covered in more detail later on. There will be some variance from car to car as to how easily they swirl, how difficult it is to correct and some colors, such as Black, simply show all the defects much more clearly than a lighter color would. For example, a Mercedes-Benz typically has a very "hard" clear coat. This means that it's more difficult to swirl the paint, but also, more difficult to correct. Then you have something like a Ford that may have very "soft" clear coat, allowing the paint to be swirled more easily, but also is easy to correct.

Now, to address another common thought: Wax does not remove swirls. Wax and sealants will simply "fill in" the swirls. Literally burrowing themselves into the valleys of the swirls. This can give the illusion of a perfect finish, but take some isopropyl alcohol and a cloth, wipe an area down and magically those swirls are back with a vengeance! Some people know this full well, but settle for "good enough". Well, you love your car, so do I, thus you and I won't settle for "good enough", right?

Car Washes: Perfectly safe, why bother doing it the hard way? Just use the sprayer, not the brush and you'll be fine?

Again, common ideas, but incorrect. We'll start with why car washes are NOT perfectly safe. Picture for a moment an average drive-through carwash. Convenient, cheap, simple. Right? Just drive up, throw it in neutral and let it do all the work.

The problem? The design of the carwash itself and everyone before you. The various brushes, flaps, and other moving parts that come into contact with your vehicle were designed using averages. What is the "average" pressure and amount of contact that is needed to clean "most" cars? The result is a very forceful and damaging amount of pressure that can lead to dings, dents, antennas being snapped off and the dreaded nuisance of swirls, which leads to the next point. Everyone before you. They wanted that same convenience and had their cars washed there, too. So the crud, grime, and debris that WAS on their car, is now on the washing devices and now it's on YOUR car. All of this grit and grime is now in the bristles and flaps hammering against your car, grinding into the paint. That is why in the detailing world, these car washes are affectionately called "swirl factories".

So take your more common bay wash: safer, right? Just don't use those horrible brushes? Also wrong. While the bay wash is safer overall, assuming you do not use those manual brushes (please don't), these car washes are in it to make money like everyone else. So, the soap they typically fill their reservoirs with, which is being sprayed on your car is rather low quality and overly strong. These soaps normally contain tons of phosphates and salts. While they do clean and get the job done, they are very harsh on the paint and will strip wax or sealants to some degree off the paint.

Assuming the car hasn't been sealed yet, or is extremely dirty (like a truck that's been off-roading or a car subject to a ton of salt spray from wintery roads), a blast from these high-powered hoses is not a bad idea before you hand wash. Or you could pick up a power washer and have similar power yourself. Just be aware that these methods by themselves will not lead to great results.

Drying Methods: Grab a good 'ole chamois? A bathroom towel?

Drying is an important topic to cover, as this "stage" of the process is where 80% of paint defects such as swirls, scratches, and water spots are introduced. How you dry the car will also depend on which washing method you choose. These two topics will be covered in depth later in their respective chapters.

However, I wanted to address some questionable choices of drying aids. For a long time, the chamois has been the go-to of many old school hot rodders and enthusiasts. It's a peculiar piece of leather essentially, that is sometimes incredibly stiff when bone dry, but is very absorbent and pliable when wet. The absorbency is what attracted these folks to use it in the first place. The issue lies in it being leather. The absorbency is great, but it lacks any sort of fibers to clean the inevitable mineral deposits left in the water droplets. So you're left with a dry surface but tons of water spots, which are the leftover mineral deposits that were sitting in the water droplets such as in the example below:

The second issue is when it's still in a semi-dry state, the fibers are very stiff, so introducing defects becomes almost inevitable. This leads to another common tool I've seen used to dry a car: The trusty bath towel. (Believe it or not!) The problems with using this are almost identical to the chamois with an additional concern, which is the fibers of a bath towel; they tend to have all sorts of debris cling to them. Leaves, dirt, and grit all get stuck in the fibers and that is what you are now grinding into your paint!

So throw away your chamois and keep your bath towels where they belong! (If you'd like to dry yourself off with a chamois, I can't stop you though.) The only type of cloth that should touch your paint is a quality microfiber or perhaps a terry cloth. (More on this in the Tools of the Trade and Wash Methods chapters)

Dust, Bugs, and Bird Droppings: Safe to wipe off with a dry cloth or a car duster? A good scrubbing all you need?

Imagine yourself with your car at a car show. It's looking great, except for a slight film of dust. Aggravating, right? So you whip out your trusty microfiber cloth or a car duster and give the car a once over. Dust is gone, awesome! However, (I always have to be a Debbie Downer, huh?) you did much more than remove that dust. You just introduced fine swirls into the paint. When you have a dry cloth, you have one friction point and the dust sitting on top of the paint, and then the paint itself is the other friction point. You're taking that cloth and essentially grinding that dust right on the paint as there is no product to reduce the friction or to lift the dust off the paint to safely wipe away. Car dusters are the worst offenders because of the amount of fibers hitting the car at once. These dusters are designed to be used extremely gently where the fibers barely touch the paint, however more than 90% of the time, they are used incorrectly and smashed on the paint. This is why I would strongly discourage their use.

The fix for this is simply to use some spray detailer, spray wax, anything that has polymers that will create a barrier between the two friction points and lift the dust off the paint. Liberal use is encouraged here, the better barrier you can create, the less likely you are to introduce swirls.

Now I'll invite you to step inside the "imagination-mobile" again: You've just been driving on a wonderful summer night, it feels fantastic outside. Perfect for cruising around. You arrive at wherever you were going, step out of the car and notice the awesome new bug collection your grille, bumper, headlights and hood have just made! Neat collection, but frustrating, right?

So how do you clean that mess off? Just take your microfiber and get to scrubbing? Absolutely no. Depending on if your paint has been sealed or protected using your favorite product or coating will determine how difficult those bugs are to get off. For the sake of the example, let's assume there is no sealant/coating and it's just bare paint. To remove those bugs using just a microfiber would require a lot of scrubbing as the speed, heat and biological make-up of the bug (Sorry, I'm no entomologist!) will have baked that little guy on. If you were to try to scrub away, you would be grinding not only the bug parts, but also the cloth itself vigorously against the paint, which will lead to swirls and possibly scratches. So before you scrub at all, spritz the area down with a good quick detailer (I recommend always keeping a small bottle and a microfiber in the car at all times) and let it soak for a few seconds, then gently wipe it away. If the bug is still stubborn, you may need a stronger product specifically for bug removal. Be sure to always follow the directions on the bottle, but generally you spray onto the areas, let it sit for a few minutes and then wipe away. Then make sure to spritz a bit more detail spray to mop up the rest of the product and bug guts.

Hop aboard the imagination-mobile with me one more time. (This is the last time I'll use "imagination-mobile", I swear!) You get to work and park your car under a nice shady tree, it is a hot summer day after all, don't want to come back out to a blazing hot car, right? So you do your thing for the rest of the day and now it's time to go home, finally! You walk out to your car to discover that some neighborhood birds have decided to carpet-bomb your car with their white little presents. Aside from having to calm yourself down from trying to hunt down every bird in a 5-mile radius with a BB-gun (I don't advocate violence against animals, though!), what will you do? If you have been paying attention, you certainly won't try to tackle it with a dry microfiber, right? Good! Time is a factor with bird droppings because of their diets, their poo is extremely acidic and can eat through sealants, waxes, and even the paint itself if left on for too long, leaving "etching" marks in the paint where it has dissolved the paint like in the example picture below:

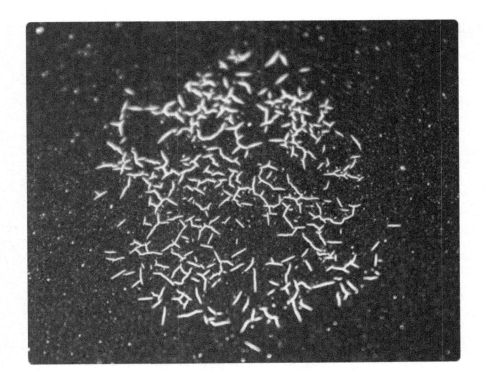

Once the rage has settled, take out your trusty bottle of spray detailer and soak the affected areas liberally. Let that sit for a few seconds in order to loosen up the poo. (Not the most attractive phrase, is it?)

After it is wet again, you can gently wipe off the areas with the microfiber. I would suggest also spraying the microfiber towel a bit before you wipe. After you've gotten the visible poo off, spray a bit more and do one more pass to ensure that all the remnants are gone. If the birds were particularly vicious to you, it may be a better option to simply wash the car.

Now that we've gone through some of the most common mistakes or challenges you'll run across, we can now get into the nitty-gritty details! (Pun INTENDED)

3

Tools of the Trade

In this chapter, we'll touch on some of the tools you'll need to accumulate apart from the obvious two: Water source and power. Don't worry about buying everything at once! I'll list them in order of importance and you can gradually build up your detailing arsenal!

Wash Buckets with Grit Guards - I suggest keeping two handy, depending on which wash method you choose to use (more on that in the Wash Methods chapter). The buckets are your normal five gallon buckets with the addition of Grit Guards. These are small plastic inserts that go inside the bucket. They have a grid screen and their purpose is to allow dirt and grit to fall to the bottom of the bucket, but not allow them to swirl back into the rest of the water so that it could end up back on your wash media.

You can also scrub your wash media against the screen to make sure it is extra clean from debris. Without these guards, you run the risk of grinding the dirt and grit right back onto the paint!

Quality Wash Media - This will again depend on your wash method choice, generally it will be a mitt, microfiber cloth or a specialized sponge (Not just any old thing under the sink!)

The first wash media is the mitt. Simple and effective. The ones I typically recommend are chenille mitts as pictured below. They have hundreds of little "tentacles" that make them exceptionally good at retaining cleaning products and soaps, as well as having great cleaning ability. They're also relatively easy to clean, provided they aren't excessively soiled.

Next we'll talk about microfiber cloths as a wash media. They are the staple and Swiss army knife of your supplies. With little exception, they should be microfiber cloths and nothing else. (Terry cloths for some specific purposes) Although, just because they are microfiber does not make them good, not all microfiber is created equally. They do come in different sizes, "pyles" and textures. A "waffle weave" towel is a good example. As the name implies, it has overlapping weaves, resembling a waffle. These are fantastic drying towels, as they are extremely absorbent. However, they won't fare very well with detail spray or trying to remove something from the paint. When shopping for quality, you'll want to skip the auto parts store and go directly to a detailer supply store or online. You'll be looking at the blend and "weight" of the towels.

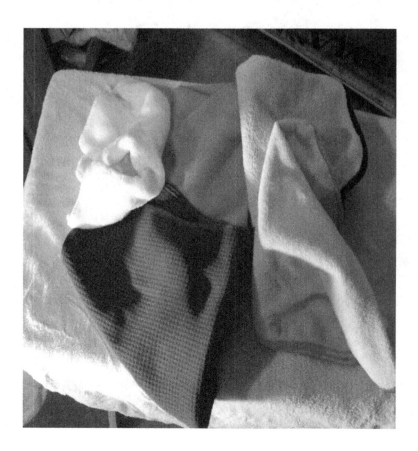

They are typically a blend of Polyester and Polyamide. So when you see a 70/30 towel, it means 70% Polyester (polyester is almost always the larger percentage of the blend) and 30% Polyamide. Polyester gives the strength and absorbency to the towel, while polyamide gives it the softer silkier texture to be gentle on the surface.

Different blends have different purposes. So an 80/20 towel is going to be very absorbent, but not as soft on the surface as a 70/30. A softer, higher polyamide blend number is typically better for buffing something off, like polish, wax, and cleaners.

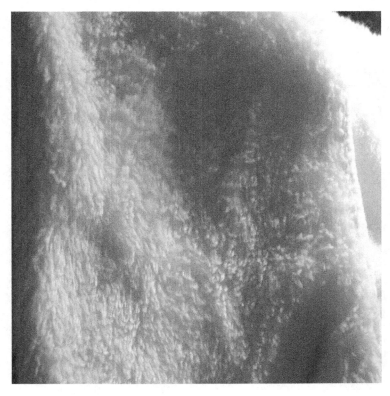

The "weight" of the towel is expressed in GSM (grams per square meter), it simply refers to how thick the towel is. Thicker towels are a bit better at buffing delicate areas such as paint, while thinner towels are better suited to less sensitive areas like wheels, doorjambs, plastics and so on. Thicker towels are also more absorbent than their thinner counterparts. We'll get more in depth at what kind of towels are suited for various purposes in their respective chapters.

Microfiber towels themselves have millions of tiny "hooks" on the end of their fibers that make them exceptionally good at cleaning a surface as those hooks gently remove contaminants off the surface. This leads to the next point of when I said "not all microfiber is created equal".

To test the quality of the towel, simply rub it against your skin. Does it grab onto your skin a bit? If so, it's going to do its job. If it doesn't, you may have a low quality towel. The next test is to bring it up to a good light source and stretch it gently. If you see a lot of light passing through the fibers, it's not well made.

Finally, a personal favorite of mine is the sponge. No, not just any old sponge like you see in the movies. This sponge was made with the detailer in mind by detailers. This one is called The Big Red Sponge, by Optimum Car Care. Unlike other sponges, its materials and construction are unique in that it has cross cut sections where dirt can be trapped rather than sitting on the surface and cleaned out very easily. Combined with a rinse-less wash (explained more in Wash Methods), it's a quick and easy pairing. With this one being the exception, I would not suggest any other sponges as they can scratch very easily.

Brushes - This can consist of brushes for the wheels, wheel wells, tires, engine bay and interior. If you get the right brushes, they can be very versatile and work in multiple areas. The only areas I would highly discourage any brush from touching is painted surfaces and glass. This can very easily cause a damage in the form of marring.

What brush you choose for wheels will depend on a couple of factors: What surface is the wheel made of? Bare aluminum, painted, chrome, or steel. How neglected or soiled are they? Heavily soiled or neglected wheels will require a more aggressive approach. Generally speaking, you would want a good firm, yet soft boar's hair brush with flagged tips. Boar's hair is very sturdy, yet with flagged bristles that are very gentle. This is especially important on painted or chrome wheels that can be marred and show it very easily.

In the case of wheel wells, you'll want firmer bristles and a long handle in order to maneuver it around in the well. This need not be any special kind of brush, just what works within the space of the vehicle.

With tires, you'll want an even firmer, short handled or palm brush for good abrasion to scrub the ground in dirt and grime off tires to prepare them for dressing later.

For the engine bay, you'll want a multi-purpose brush that is on the firmer side, but not as much as the wheel wells or tires, but one that has good scrubbing power for those grimy areas on older or neglected cars. You may need a set of different sizes depending on the constraints of the vehicle.

Interior brushes come in all shapes, sizes and qualities. This is another area where you'll want to invest in a variety. Investing in good quality horsehair brushes will ensure they last quite some time without shedding bristles all over the interior of your vehicle. Which brushes and what sizes you will need will depend on the vehicle. In general, you'll want a couple different sizes of soft bristle brushes for vents and crevices, a good firm carpet brush for carpet and mats, a slightly softer version for cloth seats and if you happen to have special seat material like Alcantara or suede, a brush like the one pictured below does a treat to fluff up the fibers while releasing trapped dust and dirt.

Drying Aid - This can be either an air compressor or even an electric leaf blower.

Not everyone has access to or can afford a compressor and attachments, so a good alternative to help get water out of cracks and cervices is an electric leaf blower. I say electric specifically because gas powered blowers produce exhaust, which then sticks to paint. A simple $30 leaf blower from the hardware store can be a great help in drying the car and getting water out of nooks and crannies that are very difficult to get by hand.

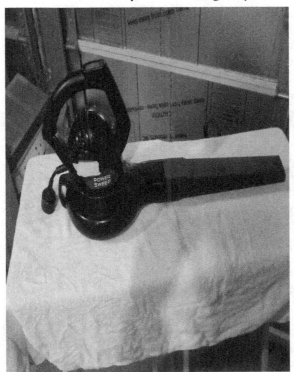

Vacuum - A good wet or dry shop vacuum is essential for good interior cleaning.

It need not be a high-end detailing vacuum; you can get a simple shop vacuum for $40-$50. Having the wet or dry variety makes this far more versatile. Be sure it has good peak power and from a reliable brand. A bunch of attachments are handy, but not necessary. The standard rake shape and narrow nozzle is perfectly fine.

Dual Action Polisher - Essential for most paint correction along with the proper pad and compound or polish.

For a bit of distinction, dual action polishers, orbital buffers, and rotary machines are all different machines. A rotary and orbital buffer use what is called "forced rotation" meaning that they spin with great force in one direction. In the right hands, they can correct extremely quickly, however, in the wrong untrained hands, they can wreak havoc. I find the Griot's Garage Dual Action polisher a solid choice for a beginning machine. Good power, great reliability, and excellent usability. You can get away with a cheap machine from Harbor Freight or a similar store, though.

Forced rotation's major downfall is heat and friction build up in one area, which if left for too long or with the wrong technique can leave "buffer trails" or holograms in the surface of the paint. These are very visible sections of damaged clear coat from improper use. They can even lead to "burn through" in extreme cases. Burn through is when enough friction is built up to literally wear through clear coat and into the base color leading to a clear/brownish spots. If paint gets burned through, it's a wrap. It will need to be re-painted. This is why I strongly advise the DIY person to skip forced rotation machines altogether, or at least pick up some junk yard parts to practice with first.

Dual action polishers address this big downfall with how they operate. Along with the rotation, the pad and backing plate oscillate in circles. This is called "throw", or how far it oscillates from dead center. More throw typically means more correction area. Because of this oscillation, it distributes heat and friction far better than forced rotation. They are also equipped with a safety clutch, meaning; if you press down too hard or it hits a threshold where it may start causing damage, the clutch engages and the rotation stops. The oscillation continues, but without the rotation, there is no correction being done, thus no chance of damage.

The downside to the dual action polisher or DA, is because it does oscillate; it has less correction power, so correction will take longer and it doesn't have quite the power of a forced rotation machine. The safety and learning curve being so good is why it is the best choice for the DIY person.

These machines are able to be set to various speeds for different jobs. Lower speeds are usually reserved for sealants or waxes, while higher speeds are used for paint correction.

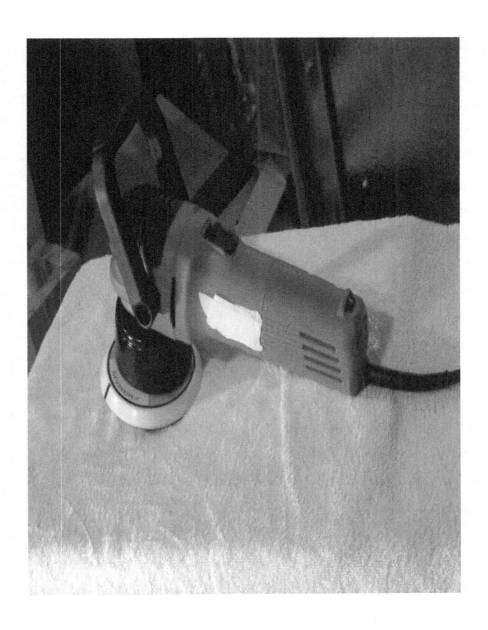

Polishing Pads - Along with a good polisher and product, essential for paint correction. You may also grab a pad cleaning tool in order to keep them clean.

Polishing pad is a very broad term consisting of hundreds of different materials, thicknesses, sizes and uses. However, for the sake of what I'm trying to teach, I'll keep it simple to what you're most likely going to need.

When I mention different materials, most of the pads you'll come across will be made of foam. There are different materials, but you need not worry about them just yet. Each type and consistency of foam will have different purposes, however, thankfully the manufacturers typically color code the pads to their use. For example, a black pad may have little to no cut at all and may just be for sealants/waxes. A white pad may have very little cut and may be for jewelling, a yellow may have a bit more cut and be used for finishing polish, while an orange will be a medium cut and be meant for the brunt of the polishing work and so on. The colors are not universal, so consult with the pad manufacturer to know what each color is made for. They also suggest an optimum machine speed for each pad and purpose.

Pad thickness comes into play for how much "give" the pad has in what it is doing. The pad is designed to absorb some of the shock of the rotational force and to contour to the panel you're working with. However, the thicker the pad gets, the more of the shock it absorbs, but the less correctional force it's exerting. Most polishing pads are about 1.5" thick for a good balance of contouring, shock absorption and correction ability. Some pads have a closed cell back for a firmer pad for more correction ability.

Pad size is mostly important because of the size of the area you are working with. A larger pad, a 6.5" pad for example, may be best used on large, flat areas for a large correction area. However, it may prove rather useless for a small angled section, where a smaller pad like a 4" may be a better choice. The secondary factor is that the smaller pads have a bit more correction ability as the machine produces the same force, but it requires less force to move the smaller pad and backing plate, so more of the force can be directed onto the surface. A larger pad will have a larger working area, but less correctional force. For most surfaces, it's about finding a happy medium like a 5.5" pad. However do not neglect the various curves and angles of your vehicle to plan out what sizes you may need to efficiently correct it.

The backing plate is also an important consideration as you want one smaller than the pad itself to reduce the chance of the actual backing plate hitting against the surface. So for example, on a 5.5" pad, you would want a 5" backing plate at most. However, you don't want one too small that the pad folds over. So 4.5" is as small as you'd want to go. If you have more angles and contours, you may want to opt for the smaller 4.5" plate to have a good "lip" of pad.

Lighting - Also essential for paint correction to view the defects and see progress of your work.

Various types of lighting can be used so that you can inspect the paint work for defects and track your progress as you correct the paint. Typically, the best type is intense LEDs that have one single diode for the best view. (If you look at the lens of a LED flashlight, swirl finder light or shop light, you can see if it's one large diode or a cluster of many.) However, don't discount the good ole halogen shop lights. Sometimes a halogen light can produce a different lighting that may capture defects, which the LED doesn't. It can even go as far as using various colors of lighting to get different views, but for our purposes, we will stick to basic LED and halogen lights.

Nitrile Gloves - These are a safety and convenient piece of equipment. With some of the chemicals we will be using, these can dry or crack your skin, perhaps even burn. So you will want protection for your hands. Gloves can come in latex, rubber or nitrile. I would recommend nitrile over the other two, especially if you have a latex allergy. These can be found just about anywhere, just make sure they fit properly, not too tight to cut off circulation, and not too loose as to fall off or allow chemicals to seep in.

Masking Tape - Preferably painter's tape. This is used to mask off areas during polishing so that the buffer doesn't hit them or the polish doesn't discolor them, like black moldings or plastics.

D.I.Y. - Detail It Yourself

Steam Cleaner - This isn't necessary to have, you can even rent one rather than buying one if you need to. However, it does help in cleaning seats and carpets, especially those that may be heavily soiled. Be sure you understand how to operate it before using it and use the proper soap for it.

4

Products

A long with the proper tools, a set of quality cleaning products is essential for good results. Here, we will go over some of the categories and how to find a quality product. I will mention some specific products, however, I am not affiliated with, nor receiving any compensation from any of the companies or products I mention, these are just my personal recommendations. All product names and formulas are property of their respective producing companies.

First, we should discuss how to find a quality product. The market is absolutely flooded with thousands of products, so how do you eliminate the junk? Most do this by picking a product and testing it out for themselves; while this is a good method, it obviously can get aggravating and expensive. With few exceptions, most products you find in your local auto parts stores are junk. They're watered down, weak, and cost more over the long run than getting the right product for the job the first time. The best course of action is to either start with my recommendations or go online to a detailing supply site (there are many good ones I'll mention in the Resources chapter) and look at the reviews. These are generally people very serious about what they're doing. If you're fortunate enough to have a local detailing supply store, stop by and speak with the staff there. They are normally detailers themselves that can help you pick the right products for your needs.

There are also a few brands that are very good at marketing but sell overpriced and mediocre products. At the end of the day, what you choose depends on your budget and the kind of results you are looking for, however keep in mind that these processes are 70% technique and only 30% products. (But that 30% can help make it easier!) I will list only the necessary products, more specialized products for specific issues should be researched carefully before use.

As with all products I will list and in general, remember to read the label and follow instructions carefully, especially those dealing with safety and environmental concerns. Some stronger chemicals can be quite nasty to you and the environment if the proper precautions are not taken. Make sure you know what to do if you accidentally get any of these direct on your skin, eyes, nose, or mouth. With the stronger chemicals, ensure that you're in an open, well ventilated space.

1. Wash Soaps and Rinse-less Wash Products - When we're looking at soaps or rinse-less products, the primary attributes we want is dirt encapsulation and lubricity. Basically, how well it lifts dirt and grime off the surface and how good of a barrier it produces between the surface and your wash media.

Both of these factors help to make cleaning the surface easy and prevent any marring during the process by preventing the dirt or grit from grinding right against the paint or surface. All other attributes are secondary to these crucial two. It doesn't matter how well the soap suds up or how good the rinse-less wash smells, if they can't clean properly, they're not worth picking up.

Pay close attention to the details of the product when deciding on one. Some may offer lasting protection with something like carnauba wax or other synthetic polymers in the product. While this is convenient, in some circumstances when you just want fresh and clean bare paint, like before polishing for instance, it is best to have a "body shop safe" product. What it means is that cleaning is all it does. It does not leave behind any fillers, wax, polymers etc. It simply leaves clean, bare paint.

For Rinse-less washes, keep in mind that most are in concentrate form and that a little bit typically goes a long way; be sure to read the product instructions. For Water-Less washing, you can use the Rinse-less wash products with a higher dilution of product versus water. How they are used will be covered in the Wash Methods chapter.

Recommendations (Again, I have no affiliations whatsoever with the companies, these are personal recommendations that I've found work well):

- Car Soap: Pinnacle Bodywork Shampoo
- Car Soap: Wolfgang Auto Bathe
- Car Soap: Griots Garage Car Wash

- Rinse-Less Wash: Optimum No Rinse Wash & Shine
- Rinse-Less Wash: Gary Dean's Infinite Use Detail Juice
- Rinse-Less Wash: Ultima Waterless Wash Plus+ Concentrate

2. Glass Cleaners - A quality glass cleaner can be very simple, but the primary attribute is ammonia-free. Especially if you have tinted windows, ammonia can be quite damaging to the tint and interior

plastics. There are even some home remedies I'll mention to make your own glass cleaner with things you may have around the house.

Some glass products may have a water repellant coating in the formula, these don't typically last long, so I would skip them in favor of true glass coatings.

Recommendations:
- Ready to Use: Stoner Invisible Glass
- Ready to Use: Wolfgang Perfekt Vision Glass
- Ready to Use: Optimum Opti-Glass Clean & Protect

- Home Made: White Vinegar (2 cups of water (distilled or filtered is best so it doesn't leave residue), 2 tablespoons vinegar, a few drops of essential oils can be used to cut the vinegar smell, but are not necessary)
- Home Made: Baby Shampoo (3 small sized drops of baby shampoo to 32oz of distilled water)

3. Quick Detailing Sprays: A detailing spray or quick detailer is simply a spray product that is used to create a barrier between the surface and the media, a microfiber cloth for example. It contains a lubricant polymer that helps prevent marring while lifting small amounts of debris like dust off. It can also be used to "soften" a

microfiber cloth before wiping as a bit of added insurance.

The rinse-less washes I mentioned before are actually great to use for this as they are concentrated and can be diluted into a spray bottle with water to be detailing sprays. This saves a lot of money over the long run, and is more convenient.

Recommendations:
- Concentrate: Optimum No Rinse Wash & Shine
- Concentrate: Gary Dean's Infinite Use Detail Juice
- Concentrate: Ultima Waterless Wash Plus+ Concentrate

- Ready to Use: Wolfgang Instant Detail Spritz
- Ready to Use: Menzerna Jescar Paint Refresh Professional Grade Detail Spray
- Ready to Use: SONAX Brilliant Shine Detailer

4. Wheel Cleaners: There are many different wheel cleaners, some are meant for only certain types of wheels, so be sure to read the bottle carefully when choosing one for your vehicle. There are also varying strengths, depending on how soiled or neglected your wheels are, all the way up to wheel acids which I will omit from this because wheel acid is rarely necessary and without proper safety gear and a collection system, these can be harmful to you, the wheels and the

environment if used improperly.

For the purpose of the book, I will recommend quality general use wheel cleaners. Be sure to follow the instructions, as some of the stronger cleaners can stain your wheels if left on for too long, especially in heat or direct sunlight. Some cleaners actually have a chemical change that turns brake dust, iron particles and grime a reddish color to show you that it is working and how much filth there really is. This isn't a necessity, but it's nice to have information!

Recommendations:
- Wheel Cleaner: SONAX Wheel Cleaner Full Effect
- Wheel Cleaner: 3D BDX Brake Dust Remover
- Wheel Cleaner: Wolfgang Uber Wheel Cleaner

5. All Purpose Cleaners: The name says it all, these are the Swiss army knives of the arsenal! However, I tend to only recommend them on really grimy areas like wheel wells, tires, underbody, the engine bay, or perhaps on very tough spots to clean, like road tar, sap, etc. They are usually a bit too strong (unless diluted) for more delicate tasks like paint.

There are tons of products out there, so I'll split my recommendations between gentler options and then stronger cleaners for REALLY dirty jobs. Again, be sure to follow the instructions on the bottle and dilute as necessary. High concentrated cleaner on the wrong surface can lead to discoloration or damage.

Recommendations:
- Gentle: Optimum Power Clean
- Gentle: Sonax MultiStar All Purpose Cleaner
- Gentle: AMMO Citrus AP Cleaner

- Strong: Simple Green
- Strong: Purple Power
- Strong: Meguiar's Super Degreaser D108

6. Interior Cleaners & Protectants: Interior cleaners come in a wide variety depending on the surface to be cleaned. A plastic or vinyl cleaner may not be the best idea for leather and vice versa. Protectants are the same way, these products are designed for specific purposes and should be used as such. (Read the label! Getting tired of that one yet?)

I'll break each category out into common surfaces for reference. For any interior cleaner or protectant, remember to choose a small test spot that is hard to see, just to check for any discoloration that might occur.

Recommendations:

- Plastic/Vinyl Cleaner: Einszett Cockpit Premium
- Plastic/Vinyl Cleaner: Optimum Power Clean
- Plastic/Vinyl Cleaner: Meguiar's Vinyl and Rubber Cleaner and Conditioner M40

- Leather Cleaner: 303 Automotive Leather 3 in 1 Complete Care
- Leather Cleaner: CarPro Inside Leather & Interior Cleaner
- Leather Cleaner: Leatherique Prestine Clean

- Carpet/Cloth Upholstery Cleaner: 303 Spot Cleaner
- Carpet/Cloth Upholstery Cleaner: Sonax Upholstery & Carpet Cleaner
- Carpet/Cloth Upholstery Cleaner: Optimum Opti-Clean

- Plastic/Vinyl Protectant: 303 Automotive Protectant
- Plastic/Vinyl Protectant: Meguiar's Plastic and Vinyl Coating D45
- Plastic/Vinyl Protectant: Blackfire Interior Protectant

- Leather Protectant: Lexol Leather Conditioner
- Leather Protectant: Connolly Hide Care Leather Conditioner

- Leather Protectant: Leatherique Rejuvenator Oil

- Carpet/Cloth Upholstery Protectant: 303 Fabric Guard
- Carpet/Cloth Upholstery Protectant: Gtechniq I1 Smart Fabric
- Carpet/Cloth Upholstery Protectant: Optimum Carpet & Fabric Clean & Protect

7. Compounds and Polishes: These are broad terms referring to products that are working with the pad to produce correction on the paint. They have varying degrees of abrasives in order to level the clear coat or paint to remove imperfections. They are generally broken up into Compounds, Polishes and Finishing polishes. Compounds being the most aggressive and needed in more neglected or extreme cases and getting progressively gentler.

It is important to start with the least aggressive option first and get more aggressive as necessary. Going too aggressive can actually cause damage and then you'll have to "step down" to remove the damage. For example, if a car has minor swirls and you use a heavy cut compound, you could end up doing even more damage. You will then having to use a medium cut to remove that damage, then a light cut to remove that and the original damage when you could have gotten great results by just using the light cut to begin with.

Pad cleaner is also necessary to help remove polish and compounds from your pad so that it works 100% after doing a few panels.

Recommendations:

- Compound: Menzerna Heavy Cut Compound 400
- Compound: Meguiar's Ultra-Cut Compound M105
- Compound: Rupes Zephir Gloss Coarse Gel Compound

- Polish: Griot's Garage BOSS Correcting Cream
- Polish: CarPro Fixer
- Polish: Menzerna Medium Cut Polish MC 2500

- Finishing Polish: CarPro Reflect Polish
- Finishing Polish: Menzerna Super Finish Plus 3800
- Finishing Polish: Meguiar's Ultra Finishing Polish M205

- Pad Cleaner: Blackfire Advanced Pad Cleaner
- Pad Cleaner: Wolfgang Pad Werks Polishing Pad Cleaner

8. Decontamination Products: There are two general categories of contaminants on the surface of the vehicle that might be left behind after a normal wash. Ferrous, or metallic industrial fallout, things like rail dust, iron deposits, construction fallout, etc. and other

contaminants like tar, sap, paint overspray and so on.

No one method will get rid of both, so we join two forces to get rid of them all to make sure that the bare paint is nice and clean before we polish or apply protectants or coatings.

The first is an iron remover; this is typically a chemical spray that adheres to iron deposits and dissolves them safely without harming any surface of your vehicle. They tend to have a chemical reaction that changes the color so that you can visibly see the chemical working and exactly how much fallout there is.

The second is clay or clay-like products; that with the help of lubrication from a clay lube or detail spray will help to shear off contaminants stuck inside the paint gently with minimal damage. They come in two varieties, actual detailing clay, which looks more like modelling clay and a synthetic rubberized towel or mitt to mimic the clay. Both have their pros and cons we will discuss in the Decontamination chapter. They also have varying "grades" from Fine or Very Fine to Medium, and Heavy. Depending on how neglected the car is, you may need to get more aggressive to remove them. Again, it's best to start from the least aggressive first, as heavier grades can mar the paint and will need to be polished out.

Paint prep products is also important in order to strip waxes, sealants and remove any oils before paint correction or adding protection. Using a normal dish soap as your wash soap beforehand will also help in removing these. As a quick note, IPA (isopropyl alcohol) diluted down to about 5-10% is great for removing oils, waxes and some residues in a pinch!

Recommendations:

- Iron Remover: CarPro Iron-X
- Iron Remover: Sonax Fallout Cleaner
- Iron Remover: Optimum FerreX Iron Remover

- Detailing Clay: DI Accessories (Fine/ Medium/Heavy)
- Detailing Clay: Clay Magic (Fine/ Medium/Heavy)
- Detailing Clay: Optimum Opti-Clay (Fine/Medium/Heavy)

- Clay Substitute: NanoSkin AutoScrub Towel or Mitt (Fine/Medium/Heavy)
- Clay Substitute: SM Arnold Speedy Surface Prep Towel or Pad (Fine/Medium/Heavy)

- Paint Prep: CarPro Eraser
- Paint Prep: Optimum Paint Prep
- Paint Prep: Gtechniq PW Panel Wipe

9. LSP (Last Step Products): These are Waxes, Sealants, & Coatings. These are what provide protection to the paint and provide hydrophobic (water beading and sheeting) properties. We'll go more into depth on them in the "Exterior Protectants" chapter.

As a brief overview, waxes are typically paste or liquid forms of carnauba wax. This is a natural wax derived from the carnauba palm's leaves. Sealants are man-made synthetic polymers that bond with paint and provide a layer of protection. Coatings are typically ceramic based, but can differ from one to another. These are specially designed to have a very strong bond with paint and have extreme hardness. Some coatings are not available to the public and must be installed by a certified detailer. The ones I list can be done yourself with proper care.

Recommendations:
- Wax: Collinite 845 Insulator Wax
- Wax: Menzerna Color Lock Carnauba Wax
- Wax: Pinnacle Souveran Paste Wax

- Sealant: CarPro Reload Spray Sealant
- Sealant: Menzerna Power Lock Polymer Sealant
- Sealant: Klasse High Gloss Sealant Glaze

- Coating: CarPro Cquartz
- Coating: 22ple HPC High Performance Coating

- Coating: Optimum Gloss-Coat

10.Tire dressing/Trim Protectant: With some trim protectants, they can double as tire dressings and vice versa as they are typically very similar surface types. These will add depth, add needed moisture to the pores of the surfaces, and most importantly protect them from sun damage and the elements.

These can be applied using a cloth, but for the tires, I recommend picking up a specific applicator sponge to make it a bit easier.

Recommendations:
- Dressing/Protectant: Optimum Opti-Bond Tire Gel
- Dressing/Protectant: CarPro PERL
- Dressing/Protectant: Meguiar's Hyper Dressing D1705

5

Determining What Your Vehicle Needs

Now that we have a good grasp on the tools and products we will need, we can move onto an assessment of what your particular vehicle will need, depending on what your goals are and how to prepare. This chapter is crucial for you to know exactly how aggressive you're going to need to be and how much time you're going to be looking at. Having a game plan ahead of time will save you a lot of frustration!

First, we look at the vehicle as it sits. What is its condition? Is it just a bit dusty in the garage, or is it filthy with dirt, road salt, mud, and so on? Has it been sitting around awhile, neglected? Is it an older car that may have single stage paint or delicate areas? Now we have the first piece of the puzzle. So, let's take a closer look from top to bottom of the car's exterior: Is there anything out of the ordinary that may not wash off that we may need to address later on? Road tar, burnt rubber, tree sap, bug guts, water spots, swirls, scratches, dents, paint transfer or red rust-like spots are all the things to take note of, as they will require special attention. Then, it's time to take a look at the interior. What is it's condition? Look for dirt build up, crumbs, stains, the stray French fry or two (as tempting as those are, just throw them away!)? Make note of anything you know you won't be able to vacuum or wipe off. The attention to detail will develop over time, especially as you learn your particular car's various nooks and crannies. The more thorough you are here, the less likely you'll be in for a surprise later!

Next, you'll get to flex your imagination muscles a bit. What do you want the final product to look like? Do you just want it cleaned up and presentable? Immaculate? Show worthy? This, in conjunction with its current state, will determine about how much time and work you're going to need to put into it so that you can plan accordingly. For example, if the car's in good shape and you simply want to get it cleaned up, it may take you an afternoon, whereas if the car has been neglected a bit with swirls, scratches and heavy soiling, it could take you all weekend (possibly more).

D.I.Y. - Detail It Yourself

Now, the phase I call "The Debbie Downer". What's going to be realistically possible? How much time do you really have? What's the weather going to be like? If it's raining or below freezing, those are obviously not optimal times. Do you have all the necessary tools and products to get the results you want? If you want those spectacular results, I would suggest waiting until you have all your ducks in a row as far as time and tools/products are concerned. However, just remember that you don't need to do absolutely everything back to back. For instance, you can do the exterior one weekend, and the interior another if one or both needs special attention. If you try to fit too much in all at once, you may over work yourself or end up with sloppy results because you rushed the job. Unlike a professional detailer who does this for a living, you may not have the luxury of going all day back to back.

We now need to have a "plan of attack", so to speak, for what you want to do. How are you going to divvy up the tasks between stages or days? I've written the following chapters in the order I usually go through, although keep in mind that you may not want or need to do absolutely everything for your vehicle. In cases like polishing, you should only do so when the car requires it, which should not be often at all if maintained properly.

At this point, we have a solid plan. You know what your car needs, what results you want, and how you're going to get it done! The last bit before getting to work is preparing your work area and getting ready for

58

action! First, start out by considering every tool, product and machine you will need. I like to lay my products and equipment out on a table in the order I'm going to use them. As you can tell, I'm a bit anal retentive, however my method works! Next, make sure you are comfortable. If you're cold or if you're sweating or if the clothing is binding up, this will cause distraction. Also, be sure to remove or be aware of anything that may accidentally scratch the car or make dings like keys, belt buckles, anything large in your pockets, zippers on the outside of clothing and so on. Finally, before you start work, stretch! As silly as it may sound, you'll be doing some physical work here. Bending, stretching, stooping, even more so when polishing with a decently heavy machine. Stretching will help make sure you are comfortable and don't tweak something too easily.

6

Wash Methods

Now we have to do some actual work! Also, this is where you will make a decision on which wash method you choose. Firstly, I'll list out the methods and give some pros and cons along with how they are done and you can decide for yourself which fits you best to continue on with the other chapters. This will also be the bulk of the labor in many cases, aside from lengthy polishing sessions, so be prepared to work!

While there are more than one ways to skin a cat, so to speak, (please, don't harm any cats!) the methods can generally be broken up into three main categories: Two Bucket Method, Rinse-less Wash and Water-less wash. There are minor variations between those, but to keep things as tidy and easy to understand as possible, I will use what I have found to work best. Now, to explain each method along with their pros and cons.

Two Bucket Method - By far is the most common and "tried and true" method you will see being used. As the name implies, you would use two buckets. One for the soapy water and one with clean water for rinsing out the wash media so that you do not contaminate the wash bucket with any grit or dirt that may be on the mitt you are using.

Having the grit guards I mentioned in the "Tools of the Trade" chapter is essential here to prevent any grit from flowing back into the main area of water and sticking to the mitt, which you will be swiping across the car. I would suggest that you do not attempt this without them. Remember, we're trying to prevent as much damage as possible, it will make your life easier in the long run, along with a better end result.

How does this method work? First, make sure you are in a shaded area as direct sunlight will make for a high potential of water spots using this method, then you would fill your two buckets with water but leaving a bit of space because the water will shift as you dunk your mitt into it. Then, following the instructions on the bottle, add your preferred soap to the soap bucket and "stir" it by spraying water into the bucket. Now, raise the windshield wiper arms up (there can be a surprising amount of dirt on these, and it gets them out of the way), then remove any solid material that may be on the car like twigs, leaves, etc. Next, we pre-rinse the entire car with water from the hose sprayer, being as thorough as possible out the exterior, inside the front grille, on the wheels and tires and up into the wheel arches. Don't be afraid to spray the underbody if possible either, especially if you live in an area with a lot of salt on the roads.

With everything rinsed off, we move on to the "sheeting rinse". Remove the sprayer from the hose and allow the water to flow out of the hose, starting at the top of the car and notice the water "sheeting" downwards, picking up the smaller beads of water along the way. Do this all the way around the car from the top of the car and let gravity do the work. As I mentioned, you would be using the chenille microfiber mitt with this type of wash, so now is the time to drunk the mitt into the soapy water a bit and get it nice and sudsy. Starting at the roof, wipe with the mitt in straight lines with gentle pressure (NEVER in circles). You may need to do one half of the roof, then go on the other side of the car to get the other half. You'll be washing from the top to the bottom, as typically the bottom panels are the dirtiest. When I say "panel", consider each part of the car: Roof, pillars, each piece of glass, door, fender, hood, bumper etc. as a single panel. After one panel, flip the mitt to the opposite side and do one more panel, after that make your way to the rinse bucket and swirl the mitt around in the water to cleanse it. If the mitt is heavily soiled, you can gently scrape it against the grit guard in the bucket. Also, if the car is heavily soiled, you may need to rinse more often. Remember to use common sense and your best judgement here.

Return to the wash bucket and sud up the mitt again and repeat the process. An important note is that when you get to the wheels, I would suggest not using the mitt on them, as it can pick up brake dust into the mitt, which is metallic or ceramic in nature and very hard to get out of the mitt, so there is a high likelihood of that ending up grinding into paint later. You can use either another mitt that is specifically designated for the wheels, the wheel woolies or brushes I mentioned in the "Tools of the Trade" chapter. If the wheels are heavily soiled, now would be an excellent time to use you preferred wheel cleaner and follow the directions on the bottle on how to use it.

Waiting for the wheel cleaner to do its thing is a great time to clean the tires using a cloth with all-purpose cleanser. Fold the cloth into fourths and spray some all-purpose cleanser, or APC for short, onto the cloth. Wipe with firm pressure starting on the face of the sidewall and then going a bit inwards onto the contact surface. Flip the towel to a clean side after each tire. Then, once the tire is wiped down, you can use that same cloth flipped inside out to new, clean sides, with a bit more APC sprayed on to tackle the inner wheel arches. Alternatively, you can use a wheel arch brush as mentioned with a bit of APC sprayed into the arches, whichever you prefer.

Once each panel and the wheels have been addressed, it's time for the rinse. Re-attach the sprayer back onto the hose and thoroughly spray down the vehicle starting from top to bottom. For the wheels, tires and wheel arches, it may take a bit to fully remove all of the product from those areas. Be sure to pay attention to the nooks and crannies that soap might hide in, like windowsills, side mirrors, taillights, plastic trim, and so on. Once all of the soap and product has been removed, we move onto the final rinse. This will be another "sheeting rinse", as before, remove the nozzle and start from the top of the vehicle and allow the water to sheet off. At this point, you can turn off the water and put the hose away. To empty the buckets, make sure you know your city ordinance for disposal, however each soap that I recommend is VOC compliant, non-toxic and bio-degradable. I typically use the leftover water to water plants or grass around the yard so that it doesn't go to waste.

This next part is optional, but to clean your engine bay is highly encouraged at least two or three times a year. Not only does it look better, it's easier to work in, and the components don't get clogged with debris (belt pulleys like to get grit between bearings!). Washing the engine bay can be a bit intimidating, but especially with modern cars, it's very safe! The engine bay of a modern car is well designed to resist water penetration to any key components like electronics. On older cars with exposed distributors, carburetors, etc. you should take more care, however. I would advise skipping the water and applying the degreaser by hand with the cloths and or/brush and wiping it off.

All you will need is a hose with a sprayer, degreaser (diluted to a light mixture like 1:10, too strong may etch some aluminum components or discolor black plastics.), a brush, some cloths, and a protectant if you so choose. I would advise against using a pressure washer, but if you have to, use very low pressure.

If you have any exposed electronics, wiring, air filters, alternator, etc. cover those with a plastic bag just to be on the safe side. You may also check that all caps, fuse box lids, and hose connections are solidly connected and nothing is ajar or loose for water to seep into. (An ounce of prevention!) Be sure that the engine has had time to cool off if it has been driven recently; you want it be cool before you begin. Also, cover the bottom section of the windshield with a towel or something else to absorb the water you're going to spray.

Begin by lightly spraying around the engine bay and the underside of the hood. Once the area is a bit wet, you can start misting the degreaser around the bay and underside of the hood. Try to get decent coverage, but it doesn't need to be saturated, a little goes a long way. Allow this to dwell for two to three minutes.

Agitate the solution with the brush or a cloth, being as thorough as you can and paying special attention to heavily soiled areas. Don't forget the underside of the hood! Lightly rinse off the entire area and check for any remaining trouble spots and spot check these as necessary. Then, completely and thoroughly rinse off the area.

You can use compressed air or the leaf blower to blow away any pools of water and help dry the area off. Next, dry with your cloths as best as you can. Remove any plastic bags or coverings you put on to protect any sensitive areas and dry those as well. (Be sure these are ALL removed before you start the car.)

You can now either, start the car and leave it to idle for 4-5 minutes to help dissipate any more water or, add your preferred dressing/protectant. You will want to use something that is not overly oily or use too much product as it can be burned off with a hot engine and smells quite bad. Use the protectant on your plastics and use it sparingly.

Now comes the drying phase: (As a quick note, at this point is really when all of the different wash methods will converge, so the information from here on is applicable to them all minus blowing water out in the case of Waterless Washing. Refer back to this point for the other methods.) Take the leaf blower or air compressor and starting at the top of the vehicle, work your way down blowing away as much water as you can. Pay special attention to easy to miss areas like the side mirrors, wheel arches, wheels, and glass sills. Once you're confident that there are no other areas that might need attention, grab a large waffle weave towel and spray it down liberally with the detailing spray of your choice. Not enough to make it "wet" but just a bit moistened. Now fold that towel into fourths. Starting at the roof again, spray liberally with detailing spray and wipe in straight lines (again, circles are a no-no as they are a big contributor to swirls). You'll want to flip to a new side of the towel every 1 or 2 panels. Large panels like the hood or roof should have a clean side to themselves. Remember, once you've used all the clean sides, you can flip the towel inside out and you have another set of clean sides. Depending on how much water was left over, you may need to wring out the towel every so often so that it becomes absorbent again and doesn't streak. I recommend using a separate towel for the wheels and wheel arches due to the brake dust I mentioned earlier.

As part of the drying phase, we want to take what I'll refer to as a "door jamb" towel, which can be one that is somewhat soiled or not the greatest quality and use that for the door jambs, inside the fuel door, inside the trunk jamb and underneath the hood to clean up any water that may have accumulated there.

Once the entire car is dry, you can also add your favorite protectant to the tires and any plastic, vinyl or rubber trim pieces. Remember to follow the instructions, as they can vary from product to product. Generally, the more product you use, the shinier the finish. I personally prefer a more "natural" light finish as opposed to an overly oily one, so I use little product overall. This is up to your discretion, though. Remember to be cautious about getting any trim protectant on paint or glass, it won't harm it, but it will leave oily residue that you'll want to clean off.

Then, we move onto the glass surfaces. Again, we'll be going panel by panel, which in this case would be each pane of glass, splitting up the rear glass and windshield into halves because of the size of each pane. Using a low-nap glass towel and your choice of glass cleaner, spray enough to get good coverage on the glass, but not so much where it's running down. A little bit goes a long way here. Take the towel and wipe along the edges, working your ways inward towards the center. Then you can take a second towel and go side-to-side and up and down to remove any possible streaks or left-over cleaner. Finally, you can take one of the towels and spray a bit of cleaner on the towel and take it to the windshield wipers. Pinch the blade of the wiper between the towel and wipe. You would be surprised how dirty they can be!

At this point in time, we will do a quick inspection over the exterior to make sure there are no water spots, pooled water, or spots that may have been missed and address those as necessary. Remember not to use a dry cloth for anything on painted surfaces, use a bit of detailing spray beforehand. This is also the point where you could potentially branch off into either decontamination, paint correction and protectants, or straight to interior cleaning. Depending on what results you want, you can make that decision.

Pros & Cons:

Pros:

- ➢ Thorough: The soap gets into various nooks and crannies.
- ➢ Safety: Done properly, this is one of the safest wash methods in terms of preventing defects like swirls.
- ➢ Utility: Can be combined with stronger soaps to strip waxes or sealants in preparation for paint correction.
- ➢ Use: This method can be used with very heavily soiled vehicles.

Cons:

- ➢ Water Usage: This method uses a large amount of water and can be prohibitive in areas under water usage restrictions.
- ➢ Product Usage: Typically, you will use more wash product versus the other methods.

➢ Time: This method is also generally the most time consuming.

➢ Laws: With some city ordinances, they require the water run-off to be collected or filtered out, rather than allowed to flow into the streets or down drains.

Rinse-less Washes - Another self-explanatory name and this method is the second most common and up-and-coming as product innovation advances. This particular method is the one I personally prefer to use. The general idea is to have overall less water usage and better time management using specialized products that have recently become very advanced to prevent paint defects while producing great results. Contrary to the name, my personal preference is to use a pre-rinse, just no after-rinse out of an abundance of caution.

As for the method, first you'll need to pick your poison as far as wash media is concerned. The "traditional" method is using numerous microfiber cloths, however I find this way to be wasteful and unnecessary. The second option is to use the same type of chenille microfiber mitt I mentioned earlier, in much the same way but without two buckets and soap. The third way is what I personally use and prefer: Using the Big Red Sponge I mentioned in the "Tools of the Trade" chapter. I will re-iterate that you cannot use any old sponge you picked up at the auto parts store or from under the sink. This one is made of specialized foam and cut in such a way to trap contaminants. It was purposely built for cleaning cars.

Once you have selected a method to go with, we will prepare by filling one bucket with a grit guard to about 4 gallons, leaving a bit of room in the 5 gallon bucket. Then, follow the instructions on whichever rinse-less wash you fancy for dilution ratios. For example, Optimum No-Rinse is 2.5 oz. to 5 Gallons, I typically do 2.5 oz. per 4 oz. just for a little extra insurance. Then you will mix this in the water as well as you can. Whichever wash media you choose, submerge that into the water and ideally you will want to let it soak for about an hour, or at least 15 minutes. You will also need a drying towel, I recommend a quality waffle weave for its absorbency. Also, leaving an extra cloth, mitt or brush soaking specifically for the wheels and wheel arches is a good idea.

Using my own variation on the method, I first do a pre-rinse. As in the previous method, lift up the wipers and remove any solid material that may be stuck or laying on the car. If your car's wheels are fairly dirty, you may want to go ahead and use your preferred wheel cleaner before you rinse as they typically work better on dry wheels. Pay attention to how long the label says that the product be allowed to set before rinsing. Once that is done, rinse from top to bottom thoroughly, paying close attention to heavily soiled areas like wheels, wheel arches, rockers and so on. Once this is done, we move onto the "sheeting rinse", remove the nozzle and let the water flow from the top of the roof, downwards. Continue around the entire car.

After the rinse, we move onto the actual washing. Take your media (If you're using cloths, fold it into fourths. Mitt, use one side at a time, and the same for the sponge.) and start on the roof wiping very gently in straight lines (again, circles are bad!). This may be odd to get used to at first, because you can't really visually see where you've wiped right away, so just try your best to do full sections of each panel and overlap a bit to make sure you don't miss a spot. You'll continue this panel by panel from the top downward. If you're using cloths, remember to swap to a clean side after each panel. If you run out of clean sides, swap to a new cloth and continue. For the mitt and sponge, one panel per side and then flip to the other side. Once both sides have been used, go to your bucket and gently dunk and wring it out to cleanse it. For heavily soiled cars, this all may need to be done more frequently. Use your best judgement. If it's visibly dirty, it's probably a good idea to swap sides/towels or wring it out.

After about one half of the car is done this way, I like to then dry those sections with the waffle weave I mentioned. Spritz it liberally with detailing spray to get it a bit moist and then fold into fourths. Start at the roof with straight lines and dry the panels that you have just washed. You may need to wring out the water in the towel from time to time. You can generally do one large panel or two smaller panels per clean side of the cloth.

Then repeat the wash on the other half of the car, followed by another session of drying. Now I normally take the extra cloth, mitt or brush I have been soaking for the wheels and wheel arches and wash those separately to avoid cross-contamination and using yet another separate towel to dry them gently. I do this with or without having used wheel cleaner first, it gives that little bit of extra cleanliness and pop. You can use those same towels to clean the exhaust tips as well!

A quick note about the rinse-less washes is that after you're done, you can actually keep the mixture in the bucket to use again, provided it isn't heavily soiled. It's best to get a lid for your bucket or something to cover it to prevent debris from falling in. With the Big Red Sponge, it's actually advisable to leave it in the bucket submerged in that solution to "live" in it. You can clean it when it becomes soiled with some APC (All-purpose cleaner) and water.

Now you can reference back to the "Drying Phase" onwards from the previous method as it remains the same with these first two methods.

□

Pros & Cons:

Pros:

> Time: Very time efficient.
> Safety: Done correctly, this method has a high safety from introducing imperfections.
> Water Usage: Very little water is being used overall in this method.
> Product Usage: Very minimal product is being used, especially if you keep the solution for multiple washes.

Cons:

> Safety: While safe, it does have room for error if done incorrectly.
> (If Using Cloths) Laundry: This will create a fair amount of laundry from the cloths used.
> Use: If the car is heavily soiled, a two bucket wash would be more beneficial.

Waterless Washes - The name is slightly misleading in that you are using liquid, just not water directly. With this method, you will be using lightly diluted rinse-less wash product in a spray bottle of your own, or you can use pre-mixed waterless washes that already come in a bottle.

I will preface this by saying that it is my least favorite and recommended method purely because of paint safety. This method should also not be used on cars that are medium to heavily soiled.

To prepare, grab your choice of waterless wash and ensure you have enough. You will be using a LOT of product, especially if you have a larger vehicle. You will also need a good amount of clean, quality microfiber towels.

Starting on the roof, fold your current cloth in fourths and then you will want to spray the product on the towel first and very liberally in the section you're cleaning. Gently wipe in straight lines as always. The difference here is; I would not recommend using one side of the cloth for more than one section or panel at a time. For example, the roof would be at least two sides, whereas a large area like the hood or door panels could be two or three. Use your best judgement and inspect your cloth, once you see it's soiled, it's time to flip to a new side. Once you have run out of clean sides inside and out, swap to a new cloth. Remember to spray your new cloth a bit before using.

With the waterless method, you will be using that one product and the cloths for the entirety of the car. If this is the method you choose, I would highly recommend designating specific towels for the wheels and wheel arches to avoid cross-contaminate your paint towels with those that may have brake dust on them.

D.I.Y. - Detail It Yourself

Pay close attention to the areas you have already covered and do a final inspection of the vehicle. As no water has been used, the nooks and crannies are likely still dirty. This is a method you can use if you're in a heavily water restricted area or have absolutely no access to outside water.

Pros & Cons:

Pros:
> Time: Extremely time efficient.
> Water Usage: Other than the water in the product, no water will be used.

Cons:
> Safety: if used improperly, this method can very easily introduce swirls and paint defects.
> Use: I would not recommend this method for medium or heavily soiled vehicles without a pre-rinse.
> Laundry: You will use a LOT of cloths and therefore have quite a bit of laundry.
> Product Usage: While you'll only be using one product, you will use an enormous amount of it for each wash.

Now that the methods have been laid out, choose the method that will accommodate your particular situation, your goals and your tolerance for error.

7

Decontamination

We come now to "Decontamination", this sounds like a term used in biohazards or hospitals, but essentially, what we are trying to do is rid the car of any particles of organic or inorganic material that has become lodged into the paint. A common example is iron particles. These are present in brake dust and industrial fallout. They can be very stubborn to remove and won't normally come off with just an average wash, so we used specialized techniques and products to remove them safely so that we can get the cleanest surface possible to correct paint or add protection. This stage also includes removing any previous wax or sealants that may be on the car already as this will impede claying or paint correction and will prevent some coatings from adhering to the paint.

If you know that there is wax or a sealant on the car already or if you are not sure, you will want to go back and wash the car (preferably with the two bucket method for this use) with a dish soap in place of car soap, use the normal procedures described in that method. The dish soap will help strip waxes and sealants off the paint. Using a paint prep or wax remover product as a follow up is also a good step to take.

To use the paint prep products, follow the instructions on the bottle. However, they will typically want the car to be fully clean and dry, then spray the product liberally starting on the roof, with a cloth folded into fourths and wipe in straight lines. Make your way panel by panel, swapping to a clean side every couple panels just to be on the safe side.

As I mentioned briefly earlier, there are organic and inorganic materials that can be embedded in paint or other surfaces. Typically, for organic material like dried tree sap, fungus spores, dried bird droppings, etc. we would use detailing clay. This clay looks much like modelling clay and comes in a variety of "grits" for whatever the situation calls for. For most uses "Fine" or "Medium" will work perfectly fine, rarely do you need to use "Heavy". With some Medium and most Heavy clays, you will introduce some micro marring into the paint, however if you plan to correct the paint next, it is not a big concern. The clay shears off the material from the surface while trapping it into the clay itself. We use plenty of detailing spray or soap as lubrication so that we don't introduce marring into the paint and so that the clay glides and can do its work rather than just sticking to surface.

How do you use the clay? First, let's make sure you've followed the first part of completely cleaning and prepping the paint or areas which you want to clay. Next, starting on the roof: Spray your preferred detailing spray liberally on the section you're working on. I would suggest an area no larger than a two foot by two foot area at a time. Tear off a relatively small piece of clay from the whole, about the size of a ping pong or golf ball should be good. Ensure that you have nitrile gloves on to help prevent the clay from sticking or rubbing off onto your skin, (this gets annoying, trust me!) spray a bit of the detailing spray onto your hands, and knead the clay like dough. Stretching it out, balling it back up, and repeat until it becomes more soft and pliable. Then you can start to flatten it a bit, not too much as to make it too thin, but you'll want it to end up around half the size of your palm flattened out. Try to make the surface that will be hitting the paint as smooth and flat as possible. If you are using the clay substitute mitt or towel, this won't be necessary, just spray it down a bit.

Now you can put the clay on the area you've sprayed down and gently glide it along the entire area in straight lines to spread out the product. Spray more product if the clay does not move freely. Once it is spread, then you can apply a small amount of pressure and glide the clay side to side in relatively quick motions, making your way from one side of the area to the other, then working down. This will look like an exaggerated "S" or "snake" pattern, overlapping each "pass". Once that is complete, do the same thing only up and down. If the car has been neglected, you will hear the contaminants being lifted off with a sound that sounds like scraping sandpaper, once the paint is clean, you'll cease to hear anything other than a bit of squeaking. If, at any time, you drop your clay onto the ground, throw it away. No ifs, ands, or buts, throw it away and grab a new piece. There are small pebbles or piece of grit that can get lodged into the clay and cause scratches or marring. If you drop a clay mitt or towel, rinse it off thoroughly and inspect it before using it again.

Once you finish one section, inspect your clay to see what you've taken off the paint (it will be surprising, I promise!). If there is anything large in it (hopefully not!), pick it out of the clay, otherwise knead the clay thoroughly again like we did to begin with and do the next section panel by panel. If you are using the clay mitt or towel, simply rinse or wipe it off after each section. You'll want to do the painted panels first, then the glass, followed by any clear plastics like headlights, tail lights etc. Don't bother with black or unpainted plastics or metals unless there are visible contaminants like droppings, bug guts, or sap. Do not use the same piece of clay or clay mitt/towel on the wheels as you did paint and make sure to do the next decontamination step BEFORE you clay them. To reiterate, if you drop your clay at any time, throw it away! (Or rinse it off and inspect in the case of clay towels or mitts)

Now that we've addressed what we can with the clay, we will move onto inorganic matters like iron deposits, rail dust, brake dust and so on. We will be using an iron removal product (refer to the "Products" chapter) to dissolve these safely. Following the directions on the bottle, spray this liberally from top to bottom of the entire car, paying special attention to wheels and wheel arches as these are collectors of brake dust. These products typically start out as a clear-ish color and slowly turn to a red color as the chemical reaction happens. Some products will need agitation with a cloth or sponge, others may not, so read closely. These cleaners typically smell horrible, so make sure you're in a well-ventilated area or wear a mask. Do not get these cleaners in your eyes or directly onto your skin.

Once the product has set for the required amount of time, it can be rinsed off. You will need to rinse thoroughly, so take your time and get in all of the nooks and crannies. Once you've completed that, you can use the "sheeting rinse" method and then dry as you would in a normal wash. (Refer back to the previous chapter, if necessary, for the steps.)

Now the vehicle is clean, contamination free and ready for yet another choice! Paint correction and then protection, or straight to protection? This is a decision I'll leave to you. I would recommend paint correction, if possible. The vehicle likely has various swirls and defects that need to be removed. Adding a protectant without correction like a wax or sealant will not remove swirls, however, they will hide them by filling them in. I would also highly discourage using any sort of semi-permanent coating without paint correction. Any swirls or defects will be "trapped" in the coating and still be visible. Removing the coating in order to go back and correct those can be a chore because of their hardness. It's best to do the proper prep-work before committing to a coating.

8

Paint Correction

For this chapter, we will discuss Paint Correction. What I mean by paint correction is removing defects in the paint so that it looks glossy, shiny and clean. I will preface this chapter by saying that there is a lot of information on this topic, so you may need to refer back to this chapter. I will try to keep it simple and applicable to most situations to give the best benefit to most of you, so there will be some elements left out such as wet sanding and paint touch up. There are, however some situations that paint correction cannot fix, or steps that would need to be taken beforehand.

So what are some things paint correction CAN fix?

- ➢ Swirls
- ➢ Light Scratches
- ➢ Light etching
- ➢ Light Fish eyes (These are small craters in the paint caused by contaminants getting onto the surface before painting. Heavier fish eyes would need to be color sanded out.)
- ➢ Holograms (These are oddly shiny spots that are caused by improper use of a rotary polisher)
- ➢ Light Orange peel (This is a common paint issue where the paint has a rough look, like an orange peel. Heavier peel will need to be wet sanded out.)
- ➢ Buffer trails (These are similar to holograms, only they are literally trails or "tick" marks where a rotary buffer was improperly used)
- ➢ RIDS - (Random Isolated Deeper Scratches. These type of scratches come from normal wear & tear and there is no pattern to them. These can show up after the first polishing step or cleaning as you get further into the paint.)

What can paint correction NOT fix?

> ➤ Clear Coat Failure (If the clear coat is peeling away, no amount of correction will make this go away. The car will need to be sanded and repainted.)
>
> ➤ Crow's Feet (This is the starting symptom of clear coat failure. This is where tiny little slivers of clear coat separate from the base coat. They look like crow's feet.)
>
> ➤ Heavy Orange Peel (This will need to be sanded out in most cases.)
>
> ➤ Deep Scratches (If the scratch is past the clear coat and deep into the base coat, these would need to be sanded out and touch up paint applied or the surface repainted.)
>
> ➤ Rock chips or Chipped/flaking paint (In these cases, the paint has been removed. There is nothing to correct. Touch up paint or a repaint would be needed.)

Now that we understand what correction can address, we can get a good idea of what the vehicle will require. The first step to correction after getting the car prepped is to embark on an initial inspection. Go panel by panel with the LED light I mentioned in the "Tools of the Trade" chapter, you may need to change the angle of the light to get a good look. What you'll likely see are small scratches called swirls. They look similar to spiders' webs. Make note of where they are, how concentrated they are and if you can tell, how deep they are. Also note any other defects you see so that we can address them.

If they can be corrected with polishing, we can usually knock them all out at once. Otherwise, you may need a more specialized technique, like in the case of wet sanding.

Next, we need to determine how aggressive we're going to need to be. The rule of thumb is; you start with the least aggressive method you feel will produce results and work your way up to a more aggressive polish or pad as necessary. This prevents any damage from being introduced from an overly aggressive approach. If the car's finish is very dull, swirled up or neglected, you may need a heavier cut polish and pad, then work your way down. If there are only a few minor swirls here and there, it'd be best to start with the least aggressive pad and polish and work up if necessary. If in doubt, start small and work up. Eventually, you're going to find what works.

The next consideration is the car itself. Not all paint systems are the same. For example, a classic that has single stage paint, has no clear coat; it's only base color coat. With these cars, caution needs to be taken with how thin the paint is. If you're unsure if it's been repainted or not sure how thick the paint is, start slow and cautious to prevent burn through. They also will have far more "paint transfer", this is literally the paint transferring from the vehicle onto the pad as it levels the paint evenly, this can be very scary, but remain calm and cautious. You also have differences in clear coats, as far as hardness and thickness. German cars typically use a ceramic clear coat that is very hard. This means it's harder to scratch and swirl, however when it is swirled or scratched, it's also much harder to correct and will require a more aggressive approach. You also have some U.S. Domestics and some Japanese brands that normally have very soft clear coat that swirl very easily, but also don't require much effort to correct. If the car has been repainted due to damage or for some other reason, it pays to know how much clear coat the painter applied, but again if you do not know: start small.

So now, what exactly are we doing when we "correct" the paint? Let's use the most common issue, swirls, as our example. When you have swirls, they are literally very thin, small scratches. If you look at a cross-section (like in the picture below), you see that the visible swirl is a dip or "valley" in the clear coat or base coat, in the case of single stage paint or deep scratches.

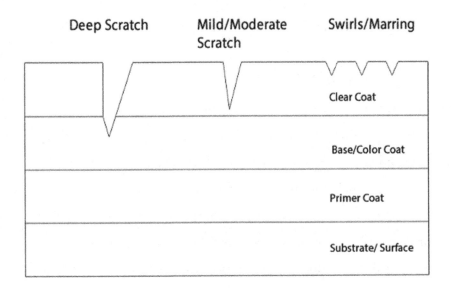

These swirls occur when something very small like dust, dirt, or other small particles get grinded into the paint, usually when you're not washing or drying the car properly. To prevent these, the surface needs some lubrication so that the dirt, dust or the wash media is not directly contacting the paint and has a layer of protection. So that could be wash product, detailing spray, and so on. Normal water is better than nothing, but it is not sufficient.

What we're doing when we polish the paint is levelling the surrounding paint so that it is now on the same plane. This might sound a bit scary, to actually be REMOVING paint, however, it is a microscopic amount in reality. When light hits a swirled up surface, the light hits the valleys and peaks of the swirls and gets refracted and bounces in several directions. This causes a dulling effect when you look at the paint. When the paint is all level and on the same plane, the light only bounces back one way, so it looks very glossy and shiny.

An important note: What we're trying to accomplish is to correct the paint once, and not have to do it again. So ideally, you can learn how to do your maintenance properly and avoid introducing any more swirls. Not only is this less work later on down the line make your car a great looking vehicle for longer, it serves an important purpose. The car only has so much clear coat, if you "burn" past it, you have paint burn through and it is irreversible and awful looking. The panel would need to be repainted. Additionally, in modern cars there is a chemical agent introduced into the clear coat that helps prevent UV light damage from the sun. When this is first sprayed, it is deep in the clear coat, but over time, it rises and settles close to the top of the clear coat. What this means is if you polish down below that point, that chemical gets released and your clear coat now has much less protection against sun damage.

In order to prepare for correction, we will need a few things: Your dual action polisher, the polishes you will need (Like Heavy, Medium and Light cut or only Medium and Light etc.), the pads you will need (Light, Medium, Heavy and the correct sizes for the panels of your car, refer back to the "Tools of The Trade" chapter to determine what sizes you may need. It's best to have at least two pads of each and some pad cleaner.), paint cleanser, detailing spray, plenty of microfiber towels, masking tape and some nitrile gloves. Also, ensure you're in a shaded area and not in direct sunlight, such as under a carport, in a garage or a pop-up tent or awning if you happen to have one of those. Direct sunlight will severely reduce the working time of the product. Nevertheless, I would highly discourage you to attempt this correction if you cannot get out of direct sun.

Begin by masking off areas of the car we do not want polished or the polisher to hit with the masking tape, such as black plastic or rubber moldings, any vents that the dust may get into. You can use the picture below as an example:

Next, put on the gloves and attach the first pad you will be using onto the DA (dual action polisher) and spray a bit of detailing spray onto the pad to help soften it a bit. This is especially important for brand new pads. On the backing plate (the part that the pad attaches to), make a small line mark with a black permanent marker that's easy to see on one side of the plate. Make sure you can still see it with the pad on. Go to the first panel to be worked on, typically the roof. Spray this down with the paint cleanser (IPA or CarPro Eraser work great here) and wipe the panel down with a cloth. Now, we "prime" the pad by taking the first polish and adding it onto the pad in an "X" pattern and smearing that around the pad with your finger. Try to get the best coverage on the pad as you can. Be sure to loop the cable of the polisher over your opposite shoulder as to keep it from smacking the car! Now add four more small drops of polish onto the pad and lightly stamp the pad onto the section you're going to work on. I recommend a section no larger than two feet by two feet. Keep stamping it onto the section until you get decent coverage. Now, turn your machine's speed setting to a low number such as two and before turning it on, put the pad down onto the section and hold it steady and firm. Turn on the machine and with very light pressure, move in an exaggerated "S" pattern (like we did with the clay) quickly to spread the product around.

Turn off the machine and set the speed setting to five (the speed of six would be used for Heavy compounds for maximum cut). Again, place the machine back onto the surface and with a firm grip, turn the machine on. The machine will be moving at a much more rapid rate of speed, so maintain a good hold on it so that it does not "walk" on you. Apply light but firm pressure, about 15 pounds of pressure, including the machine is best. You will gain the feel of this as you go. Ensure that the pad stays flat and very slowly make overlapping "S" pattern movements like before. Overlapping each pass and when you've reached the edge of your section going side to side, start going up and down. Be sure to watch that black mark we made on the backing plate earlier, this is an important indicator. If it's spinning rapidly, the machine is correcting. If it is not and is staying relatively still, then you are applying too much pressure and need to let up so that it disengages the safety clutch.

We will call each full side to side and up and down movement a "pass". Typically, you want to do at least five passes per section, more if it requires more correction. After five, turn the machine off (always turn the machine off while it's still touching the car and wait for it to stop before lifting up) and spray some paint cleaner on that section and wipe off the polish and inspect the area with your light. If the area still needs more correction, then apply four more dots of polish to the pad and repeat the process with five more passes. If it looks good with no more swirls, or the swirls have been greatly reduced (in the case of a car which needs multiple stages of correction), you can move onto the next section.

Continue section by section, panel by panel using the above

guidelines with the exception of the glass or black plastic trim or moldings. Do not use this on glass surfaces. Polishing glass requires specialized polish and pads that I will not address here. Also avoid headlights and tail lights as they are usually very soft plastic and can be damaged without using specific product and technique.

Once you have completed about two panels, it's time to clean the pad off. Use the pad cleanser and brush to remove as much polish as you can and then dry the pad with a cloth. Then you must re-prime the pad as we did initially with the "X" of polish, then smeared. Add more polish, and continue on. If you reach a point where the pores of the pad are thoroughly clogged and the cleaner doesn't seem to help much anymore, swap to a new pad of the same type and prime it. Once you have reached a point where each of the panels look good, or better (in the case of needing multiple steps), you can move onto the next stage, if necessary, or move to the final wipe down with the paint cleanser over the entire car to ensure that the polish is all removed. If you're moving onto the next stage of polishing, replace the pad you just used with the next stage and prime with the next stage polish. The process will be the same as before. If a third step is necessary after that, just repeat.

Patience will be key here to reach the results you want. If it doesn't look quite like you want, keep at it. If anything looks very odd or you see some sort of damage starting to happen for some reason, immediately stop and wipe down the area and inspect. If you can't really see the paint well but an oily surface, the polish hasn't been removed well enough yet. Some polishes are oilier, and others may be drier and "dust up" more, meaning the product will produce white dust as the product is being used.

For the final wipe down, go panel by panel and remove all of the masking tape you had put down and then wipe each panel down with the paint cleanser until you no longer see polish or the dust. Inspect in door jambs, under the hood, on the trim, in mirrors, on glass etc. for polish dust. It likes to get into all sorts of nooks and crannies. Once you're satisfied with the results and everything is cleaned up, you can clean off your polishing pads (never leave polish to dry on pads) and put everything away.

Now we can move on to Exterior Protectants, otherwise known as LSPs (Last Step Products)!

9

Exterior Protectants

When we talk about Exterior Protectants or LSP (Last Step Products), they typically fall within three main categories that tend to be lumped together: Waxes, Synthetic Sealants, and Coatings. They each have their individual pros and cons that we'll discuss along with a summary of what each of these are and what they're made of. Then, we'll look at how each of these are applied and cared for. With any of these products or methods, I would again highly discourage use in direct sunlight. The panels need to be cool for the product to bond and initially cure properly. I also would advise waiting at least for 48 hours (some products call for more) before any sort of water touches the car or the forecast calls for rain.

Waxes - Sometimes every LSP is referred to as a "wax", when in reality, wax is exactly that: wax. It is either a liquid or paste version of wax from a carnauba palm's leaves. This is cultivated and used in many products, including car wax.

This form of LSP is the most common and most "traditional", so it's what you'll often see the most. Owners of classic cars like this not just for being a bit old school, but also for the "warm glow" it gives the paint due to how light reacts with the wax.

So how do you apply wax, if you so choose to? Depending on the form (liquid or paste), you have some options. With the paste version, your only real option is by hand with a foam applicator pad. (Usually included with the wax for more quality waxes, but can be bought separately.) Be sure to follow the instructions, but generally you will light rub the applicator into the wax and then start panel by panel on a clean car (You did clean it first, right?) in straight lines, overlapping one line to the next and in the direction the wind would blow over the car. For example, on the roof, the lines of wax should be vertical facing the front of the car, or horizontal facing the side. Consider how the air will pass over that panel and apply the wax that way.

Once you finish a panel, you can take a microfiber cloth and gently buff away the excess until you get a good finish. Continue this panel by panel, making sure to avoid any black plastic or trim moldings as wax will discolor these. If you happen to get wax onto one of these areas, buff off what you can. If it won't go away, you can take a normal pencil eraser and gently work the area with it to remove the wax.

With liquid wax, you have the option of using your DA polisher on a low speed with a waxing pad, or using a foam applicator like the paste. If you use your DA, set the speed setting to no higher than two, apply a bit of the wax to a pad designed for it (they will typically be thick and a bit squishy in comparison to others). Just as we did in the paint correction stage, set the pad onto the section you're working on, then turn on the machine. With wax, you can use faster arm movement and larger working areas as you're not trying to correct anything, just spreading out the product. You could do an entire panel at a time if you wanted to. Remember to use the overlapping "S" pattern in the direction, which the wind would be passing over the car. Once you're done with a panel, buff off the excess and add a bit more wax onto the pad and move onto the next panel.

To care for a waxed vehicle, you can wash as normal, but ensure you do not have a soap that is too harsh that might strip the wax. Typically, the soaps and products will list if they are safe for waxed cars.

Pros & Cons:

Pros:

> Application: Very easy to apply.

> Cost: Most waxes are very affordable.

> Care: Easy to care for, just apply more when it wears off.

> Look: Offers a "warm glow" that is pleasing to many.

Cons:

> Durability: The least durable of the options available. You will be re-applying wax frequently in the course of a year.

> Protection: Offers the least amount of overall protection of the options available.

> Vulnerability: Harsh soaps or cleaners very easily strip wax.

Sealants - The second most common product and gaining more popularity for their versatility. These are made of synthetic polymers made of thousands of particles all linked together. They've been developed by chemists for great paint bonding and protection. They tend to give a glossy and slick look when applied.

Applying a Sealant is basically the same process as liquid wax. You have the options of using a DA or an applicator pad. (Reference above under the Wax if you need to know how to do this.) Be sure to read and follow the instructions, however. Some sealants can be difficult to buff off and may take a bit to get the finish you want.

With a sealant, you can also apply multiple coats with some products, curing times will differ between each coat depending on the product. Another option is to apply a sealant first, as your "base coat", allow it to cure, and then apply a wax so that you get the protection of two, with the warm glow of the carnauba.

As for care, sealant coated cars should be handled much the same as waxed cars. Use appropriate soap and products and they are easy to care for.

Pros & Cons:

Pros:

➢ Application: Very easy to apply.
➢ Cost: Sealants are generally very affordable.
➢ Care: Very easy to care for as it lasts much longer than waxes.
➢ Look: Offers a slick and glossy look that is pleasing to many.
➢ Durability: Durability is much improved over wax and will last several months.
➢ Protection: Offers more protection than waxes.

Cons:

> ➤ Buffing: Can be difficult to buff away excess when applying.
>
> ➤ Vulnerability: While it is not as vulnerable as waxes, some harsher chemicals can remove a sealant.

Coatings: The newest development in paint protection and a very interesting subject; coatings are by far and away the best protection you can get for your paint aside from spraying extra hard clear coat or applying a vinyl clear bra. They also offer fantastic hydrophobic properties and make the vehicle extremely easy to clean. They start as a liquid in a bottle, but once applied on a panel and exposed to open air, they start to cure and harden to a ceramic or glass (silica) based layer.

While trickier to apply correctly than waxes or sealants, they are not as intimidating as you might think. While some coatings do require a certified detailer to install, there are plenty of options for consumers.

As always, I encourage you to fully understand the process from the directions on the product, especially the time you need to allow before buffing off the excess product and the cure times. However, the general process is on a clean, decontaminated and paint corrected vehicle (All three of these are ESSENTIAL to a good coating.), you typically have the bottle of the product itself and an applicator of some sort like a small sponge with cloths, or a pad. The bottle may seem extremely small, but trust me when I say a little of this stuff goes a long way! Just a couple of drops on the applicator, apply in straight, overlapping lines gently, and spreading it relatively thin on a small section of paint at a time usually no bigger than two feet by two feet. Make sure you know how long you need to leave your particular product before you buff off the excess. Repeat section by section, panel by panel on the painted areas.

Buffing off the excess is a very important step. You may need to look at the section from different angles to make sure the finish is how you want it before allowing it to cure. If you don't buff the area properly or apply the product too thickly, you can get "high spots" which will look like discoloration in the paint. These are literally spots where the product is higher or thicker than the surrounding areas. If you do end up with some of these (You likely will if it is your first time of coating a vehicle), it is not the end of the world. You can take some light cut polish on a microfiber towel and rub that area down. This will remove the coating in that spot and allow you to re-apply the coating and try again.

These coatings are typically able to be layered, but only once each coat has fully cured. Refer to the product for cure times. You can actually have as many layers as you want, but typically, 2-3 is more than enough. However, waxes and most sealants will not adhere to the coating, so they would not be able to properly layer on top of it.

Caring for a coated vehicle is very easy but comes with some special considerations. The coating will allow for extremely easy cleaning, so you need not be too aggressive with washes. Most times with a dusty or very lightly soiled car, you can simply rinse it off with water and dry. Caution should be taken about going through drive-through car washes or using brushes or aggressive wash methods on the coating. The coating itself can become scratched or swirled if you get very aggressive or allow the large, firm brushes of a car wash to touch the car. Harsh soaps like in a touchless or self-service car wash will not strip the coating, however, I would still recommend hand washes only if at all possible.

A quick note: There are other coatings available specifically for glass, plastics, fabrics, leather, and rubber. I will not expand on them here, but there is a coating available for just about every surface type you have in a vehicle.

Pros & Cons:

Pros:

- ➢ Cost: While initially expensive, these coatings last for MUCH longer than other options, so they end up being more economical.
- ➢ Durability: By far, the most durable option. These coatings can last from one to three years. Five or more for the professional class of coatings.
- ➢ Protection: Also by far, coatings offer the most protection as they add a very hard layer of protection over the paint.
- ➢ Care: Extremely easy to care for.

Cons:

- ➢ Application: Application can be somewhat tricky and may seem intimidating.
- ➢ Defects: If any defects remain in the paint, they will be sealed into the coating. The coating would need to be polished away to reach and correct the defects.
- ➢ Prep Work: A large amount of work needs to be done to prepare for a coating to ensure proper adhesion and look.

10

Interior Cleaning and Protectants

While the exterior of the car will be the bulk of the cleaning and maintenance, to overlook the interior would make for a sub-par job. The interior can be considered the opposite side of the same coin in many aspects. Just like with the exterior, assessing the condition and surfaces you're going to be working with will be essential to a good end result.

A well-kept car interior may just need a bit of vacuuming, dusting and wipe down, while a more neglected or "lived in" interior may have stains, trash under seats, pet hair and so on to contend with.

So our first step will be to look at the surface types in the car. Is the upholstery cloth, leather, suede or some combination of those? Inevitably, there will be at least some plastics, rubbers or vinyl areas. Sometimes there may be wood paneling, either real or faux, some metal bits like aluminum or chrome. Then look at the carpet and mat material, the headliner and any other surfaces that may be a bit different. Make a list of all the types in your specific car.

Now, we take stock of the condition of everything. Remove any trash, clutter or loose items from the car and start one area at a time looking closely at the condition of everything. Is it heavily soiled anywhere? Are there stains? Pet hair? Any dry, cracked or discolored bits? (Some discoloration we may be able to remove, but some may be sun damage and will be permanent.) Be sure to make a list of this and be very thorough. Moving seats, checking the trunk and looking in nooks and crannies will be essential to a good, and thorough cleaning.

With a good overview of what we're dealing with, we can get down to business. First, if you haven't already removed the trash and loose items in the car (you should have already!), do so now. Then, remove any floor mats, seat covers, steering wheel covers, or anything that may be covering one of the surfaces we're dealing with. When removing the floor mats, try to keep any dirt or debris on the mats, rather than dumping them into the carpet. If needed, step a good distance away from the vehicle and shake the mats out.

Now, take your vacuum and get what you can off the mats initially. Then, take your carpet brush and brush from the outer edges of the mats, inwards to the center to gather debris that might be stuck in the mat. Vacuum that out and once you're satisfied that most of the debris is out of the mat, give it one more shake out and lay them in an area you can apply the carpet cleaner to (refer to "Products" chapter for suggestions). While referring to the product's instructions, spray the cleaner onto the mat and allow it to dwell for a few seconds and then agitate as necessary with the brush. The product will have instructions on how to dry, but typically, you will use a dry cloth to pat down the area. Set the mats out of the way to dry and air out.

Next, we move onto the carpet. Using essentially the same technique as the mat, vacuum the carpet thoroughly. Try to get under the seats, in crevices next to them, in the trunk, etc. You may need a smaller vacuum attachment for some areas. In the areas you can actually reach. If your car has excessive pet hair that the vacuum is not removing, use your carpet brush to help loosen it up to vacuum. Additionally, you can also use a fine grade pumice stone from a beauty supply store. Use this gently, but it works wonders for loosening up the hair. Do the same carpet brush technique as before. Pick sections to work at a time, such as the driver's side carpet, passenger's side, and so on. Work from the edged inward and vacuum the center. Once you're confident that the debris has been removed, we can move onto the actual cleaner. Again, you'll use basically the same technique and work in those same sections. Provided you have a cloth headliner, you can also use the same products to give it a quick clean-up as well. It may take a bit to pat the carpet dry, but once it's reasonably dry, we can move forward.

If there are any stains, you may need to apply extra product to that area in order to lift it. Some more stubborn stains may need more agitation with the brush. If you can determine what caused the stain, you can generally look up how it is removed chemically. Each type of stain is going to be a little bit different and unfortunately I couldn't cover every type within this book. As always, start with the least aggressive method first.

If there are any scuffs on any of the interior plastic trim, you can generally remove these with a good scrubbing with your interior cleaner. If they are more stubborn, you can try a Magic Eraser, available in most grocery stores. You will want to keep this wet and keep in mind that these can be pretty aggressive, so be gentle and I would discourage their use at all on vinyl or leather.

Before we vacuum the other areas, now would be a good time to bust out our handy interior brushes to knock dust off the various surfaces and especially the small areas we may miss while wiping, like inside vents, small nooks and crannies, info/stereo systems, around the steering wheel and gauge cluster etc. Be as anal as you'd like!

We can now vacuum out the rest of the vehicle. Start with the seats, in between the two cushions of them is where a lot of debris likes to hide, cup holders, any cubby holes the car may have, door pockets, vents, the headliner and the dash. The flat area under the back glass is a good place to vacuum as well, it likes to collect dead bugs when you have the windows down.

For most cars, the interior trim panels are some combination of plastics, rubber, vinyl or leather and these can be cleaned with many of the same products all at once. There are exceptions to that, such as suede and Alcantara where it is best to use products that are specifically designed for them, or in the case of Alcantara, soap and a damp cloth ONLY.

With two or three microfiber cloths on hand, take one and apply your preferred cleaner and spray a bit onto the cloth. With interior cleaners, I HIGHLY recommend spot testing before fully committing to wiping down. Spot testing is picking an inconspicuous small spot that's not easy to see on the panel you're working with to test the product on. This will let you know if anything out of the ordinary will happen, like discoloration, staining, or some other sort of damage. Clean that spot like you would the rest of the panel, allow to dry according the instructions and buff off. Look closely and compare with the surrounding area to make sure there are no differences. Repeat this for each of the different surfaces of your interior. If everything looks good, you can confidently mark that cleaner as "safe" for your vehicle. Remember to do this process again for a different vehicle, as not all are the same!

Once you've spot tested, you can wipe each panel of the interior. Some products will allow you to leave it as-is, others will want you to let it dry then buff off with a clean side of the cloth. Be methodical and go panel by panel so that you do not miss any spots. If any area is grimy or overly dirty, it may take more buffing with the product to clean it off.

For the seats, if they are cloth you can use the same cleaner as you did for the carpet and mats, just be sure to spot test again! You will use the same method as the carpet, be sure to use a softer brush to agitate the product on the seats, if necessary, so that you don't cause any damage. If they are leather, use your preferred leather cleaner sparingly. A little will go a long way. If the leather is cracked or very dry, it will require conditioning and protection, which we will address a bit later. If you have special seats with a mix of leather and

Alcantara or suede like in some sports cars, treat each surface as an individual. Alcantara especially, as it will discolor if you use leather products on it. It is not actually suede or leather, it is a synthetic material made of plastic fibers that mimics suede. Use only a tiny bit of soap on a damp cloth to clean this by dabbing gently and patting it dry. You can then use the special brush I mentioned in the "Tools of the Trade" chapter to fluff up the fibers.

A quick note is; if your car is heavily soiled or you like a deeper clean in the seats and carpet, you can use your steam cleaner (or rent one) on these areas for great results. Steam works very well for set-in stains or to help remove musty odors. Using the steam wand on low heat is actually effective in removing gunk on plastic panels and loosening up crud in hard-to-reach areas as well! Try to avoid using too much steam on headliners, as it can loosen the adhesive and cause them to sag in some vehicles.

Now that we have almost all of the surfaces cleaned and ready to go, we can start talking about protecting them! Wait a minute... didn't we forget about the interior glass? Yes, I did this intentionally because during the course of adding the protectants, there's a good chance you may get some of the product on the glass, so by waiting till the end, we can make sure we get that off and have perfectly clear glass.

First, we'll talk about fabric protectants, carpet, cloth seats, most headliners, the carpeted section under your back glass, and the areas in your trunk (Yes, back there!). Make sure that all of the fabric surfaces are completely dry to the touch; squish it down to make sure. If it isn't, allow it to dry before spraying any of the protectant on it. Follow the instructions for the product, as some will differ on exactly how they say to apply it, but generally speaking, it's spray on in overlapping passes until evenly wet, let cure and wipe up any overspray on any surfaces that are NOT fabric, don't let it dry on these surfaces. This protection will be very important to help prevent stains, make spills easier to clean up, prevent salt stains during the winter and even discoloration and damage that comes from UV rays of the sun!

When it comes to leather, there's actually two stages of protection: Conditioning and actual protection. Think of the leather like skin, because it is, the conditioner as lotion and the protectant as sunscreen. Without moisture of some kind, the leather dries out and cracks, much like you skin on a dry, cold day. That is where conditioner comes into play, it adds this much needed moisture to the leather so that it becomes suppler. You actually apply it much like lotion, only with a foam applicator or microfiber, working it into the leather gently and wipe away the excess. Protectant does just that, it protects the leather from spills, stains and most importantly: UV rays. Sun damage is the number one killer of leather. The protectant will be similar but will be more of a spray that you will spray onto the seat and buff in and buff off excess. Some products will actually have elements of both, so read the bottle carefully to see what you actually have. (Tired of me saying read the instructions I bet? Well it's almost over! But seriously... read the instructions!) Make sure you don't go crazy with either of the two or you will end up with a greasy, slippery mess. A little bit goes a long way! If any other surface in the car is also leather, apply this same method to those.

Finally, we have virtually every other surface: Plastics, rubber, vinyl and metals. For everything but actual metals, you can use the same protectant. For metals, I would suggest leaving them bare. If they are scratched or grimy, you can grab some metal polish and spruce them up, careful to clean up well afterwards though.

You can now pick your preferred protectant and spray onto a cloth and apply evenly across each of the panels and surfaces you need to. Most products will have a certain dry time before you should buff off the excess. Remember to use overlapping passes to ensure you don't miss a spot. Try to clean off any product if you accidentally get it on the glass as it will cause greasy streaking.

An important note however: For the steering wheel, gear shifter, emergency brake and all pedals - USE PROTECTANT VERY SPARINGLY, IF AT ALL. Having any of these bits be greasy and slippery causes a very serious safety hazard. Also try to avoid getting this stuff on your instrument cluster or any LCD/Touch screen or navigation system. With some cars, it's also best to go easy on the top of the dash as it can cause a reflection in your windshield in bright sunlight which can be a hazard.

Now, we've made it back to that glass! You can start with the easiest bits: The side windows and sunroof (if you have one) first. Use a glass cleaning towel with a bit of cleaner sprayed on it. Do not spray product directly on the glass inside the car as this can stain some plastics and vinyl surfaces and just as you did on the outside, wipe from the edges inwards to the center and then buff off. It's best to use a total of three towels for this. The first being a normal microfiber to use the product with as the initial wipe, then a second to buff off the residue, and a third, very low nap glass towel to finish it up. Be sure to open the doors, as well pinch and wipe the edges of the side windows, this is a commonly missed area.

The back window and windshield will be the tricky bits as most of the area is hard to reach. For the back glass, get what you can by sitting in the back seat or area and wipe up and down and side to side with each of the towels and for the hard to reach portion, turn your arm counter clockwise with the towel in your hand, so that your palm is facing up with the towel, and reach towards the back section that way. Optionally, you can purchase a tool like the Stoner Invisible Glass Microfiber Mop Kit (other manufacturers make a similar tool, I just happen to use this one) that will allow you to reach those areas much easier.

For the windshield, it's best to approach it from the passenger's side seat for the entire windshield, due to the steering wheel being in the way in the driver's side. Again, get what you can by normally wiping from side to side and up and down. Then you can contort your arm as you did before and do your best to get into the tight areas, or use the mop tool I mentioned earlier.

Now we're done! Do your final inspection around the interior and address anything you might have missed. Now that the car is fantastically clean inside and out, we'll work out a good plan on how to keep it this way as best as possible!

11

Developing a Regime

After all the hard work you just put into your car, you don't want it to look like it used to be again, right? I should hope not! So that's why we need to have a plan regarding how to maintain the look you have right now to the best of your ability. Some factors will be out of your control, obviously, such as your schedule, weather conditions, construction, etc.

However, we will control what we can!

☐

Generally, I recommend a full wash using your preferred method at least every couple of weeks, ideally once a week. This will normally ensure that the car is easy to clean, so that risks of any defects or damage are minimal. Pay attention to the weather forecast. If it's going to be below freezing, or it's going to storm soon, then it's best to wait till after. There is no more defeating a feeling to finish up a full detail and then feel rain or see it in the forecast, believe me! I sometimes even look at wind conditions, if it's going to be extremely gusty, then it's going to kick up a lot of dirt and dust, so it might be best to wait for it to calm down so that you can then get all that off.

This is especially important if you have road salt on the car, large amounts of bird droppings, construction dust or fallout, large amounts of water spots, or vandalism as these are all situations where you should wash your car as soon as possible so you don't allow these corrosive materials to etch themselves into your paint!

Cars that are protected are always easier to clean in general versus bare paint; however, cars coated by one of the ceramic coatings I mentioned are especially easy. Provided there hasn't been rain or any of the above mentioned nasty stuff, you can usually just rinse off the car for the most part.

Cars protected by wax will need to have a regular schedule to top off the wax every 6-8 weeks depending on the conditions, as poor conditions will take a toll on normal wax. Sealants can be anywhere between 6 months to a year. Coatings will last from one to three years from the consumer available variants.

For waxes and sealants, when it's "time" is up and you're about to top it off again, it's best to do another clay bar and iron remover treatment before you do. Refer to the steps about stripping the wax off for bare paint. If you're in a pinch, you can just top off the wax or sealant, though. Coated cars should not try to clay it, as it will shear the coating off little by little. You can still use the iron remover though. That would be best done every 6 months or so.

Cleaning the engine bay should be done at least every 6 months, especially after winter to remove any road salt or debris it accumulated.

Also, most products do have a shelf life like any other chemical. Be sure if something reaches its shelf life, or starts to smell funny, mildew, or otherwise seem expired, to throw it out. (Responsibly of course! Refer to your city's ordinances for chemical disposal.)

In order to keep your microfiber towels, cloths, mitts etc. clean and working properly for each go around, be sure to wash them properly! You can use the washing machine on "warm" but ONLY with a detergent that is "free and clean" with no dyes, fragrances, or softeners. Adding a touch of microfiber specific cleaner is also a good idea. Try to split the loads between the towels you use for paint and those that are much more soiled, like wheels, wheel wells, etc. so there is no cross-contamination. Also be aware, new towels' colors will likely bleed. If that bothers you, be sure to wash with like colors. If your white towel is now pink, it still works, though! In order to dry them, you can pat dry and leave them out to dry naturally, or put them in the dryer. However, ONLY on the lowest heat setting. Too high of heat will melt the fibers together. Do NOT add any fabric softener, sheets, or stick-in balls. Fabric softener will leave a greasy film as you use the towel. If you accidentally do this, simply wash them again to get it out.

With this information, you can plan out a detailed (Puns are fun, aren't they?) but not too obsessive maintenance routine. As you do it more and more, the time it takes you will steadily decrease as it becomes second to nature.

12

Closing

After everything we have now learned, I am confident that you are now armed with the knowledge to get out there and make the car parked outside your home look fantastic!

We've gone over:

- The most common mistakes and how to avoid them.
- The various tools you should invest in.
- The products used to make all of this happen.
- How to develop a plan of action for your vehicle.
- Various wash methods and how to do them.

- How to decontaminate your vehicle.

- Paint correction and the method for it.

- How to protect the paint.

- Cleaning and protecting your interior.

- Developing a maintenance schedule.

You can take this information with you to just about any vehicle throughout the years. Technology will continue to develop better and better products and tools, but the general ideas will remain the same!

I sincerely hope you've learned tremendously from this book and I thank you for going on this adventure with me!

As I said in the beginning, if you're a more visual learner and want to see these techniques actually applied, be on the lookout for my upcoming video course!

All of the best of luck and again, Happy Detailing!

Joseph Allen Monroe

About the Author

First of all, I want to personally thank you for picking up this book. This has been a passion project of mine and I'm thrilled that you are along for the ride!

I am a 24 year old (at the time of this writing, but let's just say I'll be 24 forever. Sounds better, right?) car enthusiast and detailer. I have been detailing for around five years as a hobby and side business. During this time, I have been privileged to have a mentor that has been detailing longer than I have been alive. (Stating the exact number of years would just be cruel, wouldn't it?) He has been a tremendous help in learning the ins and outs of detailing along the way.

I started when I bought a car I was proud of. I went out and learned everything I could get my hands on to take care of this car properly. I learned some lessons along the way and refined my craft. That is what I want to bring to you and other enthusiasts!

D.I.Y. - Detail It Yourself

I hope this book gets you started on your journey to an immaculate vehicle and the pride that comes along with doing it yourself!

Happy Detailing!

Picture Attributions

- microfibercloseup2 –

https://www.flickr.com/photos/artbystevejohnson/4776039058

http://creativecommons.org/licenses/by/4.0/legalcode

- Nitrile gloves -

https://commons.wikimedia.org/wiki/File:Nitrilhandschuhe_verschiedenfarben.jpg

https://creativecommons.org/licenses/by-sa/3.0/deed.en

- Masking tape -

https://commons.wikimedia.org/wiki/File:PaintersTape.jpg

https://creativecommons.org/licenses/by-sa/3.0/deed.en

- vacuum1 -

https://www.flickr.com/photos/jeepersmedia/14939857228/in/photostream/

https://creativecommons.org/licenses/by/2.0/

- Iron-x reaction -

https://www.youtube.com/watch?v=R67USw3uKCg

https://creativecommons.org/licenses/by/2.0/

- Car Masked off -

https://www.youtube.com/watch?v=iu50iY9RmNg

https://creativecommons.org/licenses/by/2.0/

Made in the USA
Columbia, SC
02 January 2021